Beautiful Girlhood

A Timeless Guide
for Christian Adolescence

Mabel Hale

BARBOUR BOOKS

An Imprint of Barbour Publishing, Inc.

© 2001 by Barbour Publishing, Inc.

ISBN 1-58660-260-8

All Scripture quotations are taken from the King James Version of the Bible.

Published by Barbour Books, an imprint of Barbour Publishing, Inc., P.O. Box 719, Uhrichsville, Ohio 44683
www.barbourbooks.com

ecpa Member of the
Evangelical Christian
Publishers Association

Printed in the United States of America.
5 4 3

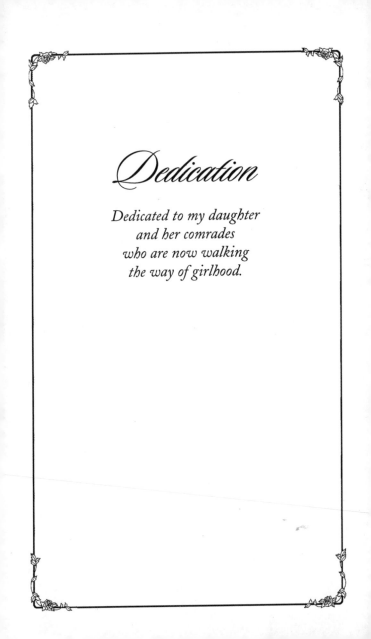

Dedication

*Dedicated to my daughter
and her comrades
who are now walking
the way of girlhood.*

CONTENTS

EDITORS' NOTE

Imagine a time before shopping malls, cellular telephones, and women's professional sports. Imagine a time when girls sewed their own clothing, played a parlor piano for entertainment, and found limited career opportunities. This is the time when Mabel Hale wrote *Beautiful Girlhood*.

What could a book from that era possibly say to girls of the twenty-first century? Plenty. Even though fashions, technology, methods of communication—society in general—have changed dramatically since Mabel Hale's day, human nature hasn't. And the underlying message of *Beautiful Girlhood*, that every girl must consciously decide to develop godly character, is truly ageless.

While some aspects of *Beautiful Girlhood* may seem quaint and dated to modern readers, there is still much to be gained from its pages. The author, in her original foreword, said,

This little book is born of a desire
to help and encourage our girls who are
struggling with the problems that come

up in teens. Youth has its problems, its heartaches, and disappointments. It is not always a smooth path to the perfection of womanhood.

If what I have written should help some girl to a nobler life and truer ideals, then I shall feel that it has accomplished the task I have set for it to do.

In the early twentieth century, many girls were guided toward Christian womanhood by Mabel Hale's words. It is our hope that new generations of girls may find the same benefit from her timeless theme.

The Editors

CHAPTER ONE

OPENING FLOWERS

Rejoice. . .in thy youth;
and let thy heart cheer thee
in the days of thy youth.

Have you ever watched the development of a rose from the tiny bud to the open flower? The bud held little more promise of beauty than the foliage about it, but day by day it grew until it was full and round. One day you saw a thread of color, promise of the rose to be, peeping through the covering of green. Each morning saw the thread of color widening until the bud burst asunder, and the flower was revealed. You looked upon this bursting bud with admiration and delight, though yet you did not see the rose in its full size and beauty. You had to wait until it was full grown and fully open, till it had reached its maturity, before you could behold the complete flower.

But in the opening blossom you had the beauty of the mature rose blended with the grace and charm of the bud.

Girlhood is the opening flower of womanhood. It has charms all its own. The wonderful change from the child to the woman, the marvelous blossoming of young, healthy girlhood, will ever be God's great miracle in life's garden. Like a half-open rose is girlhood. We are charmed, both by the beauty of the bud and by the wonderful coloring of the rose. We behold the familiar traits of childhood that have always charmed us and held our affections, but blended with these in ever-changing variety are the graces and powers of womanhood.

Do you, dear girls, appreciate the golden days in which you are living? You have your perplexities and vexations, of course, yet you are enjoying the merry, carefree days of youth, which are generally the happiest days of the whole life. You are standing "where the brook and river meet," where childhood's days and childhood's toys are put aside for the greater things of womanhood.

Girlhood's days are happy days. The blush of youth is on the cheeks and the rich, red blood of youth in the veins, while the cares of life have not yet settled upon the heart. Nature is now tuned to catch every note of music, to respond to every pleasurable emotion and fancy. Life to the normal girl is full of song and laughter. She looks forward with magic view that hides all the sorrows and terrors and reveals in bright hues all the joys and blessings. Her heart beats with eagerness to begin the conquests that will certainly be hers. From her point of view there are no defeats, no failures, no disappointments. Every thorn is hidden and every rose revealed. So contagious is her joy and optimism that her presence will cheer the dullest household and set its pulse beating with hope and laughter. Older heads, who know that life is not all joy and sunshine, come under the spell of her charms and smile with her. With garlands of hope and joy upon her lips she goes forth to meet life joyously and unafraid.

I would not chill the warmth and ardor of happy girlhood. What if I do know that the clouds and storms of life are just ahead and that its cares will bend her back and break her heart! Would they be any less if she knew? Soon enough the sorrows and pains will come. Laugh and play now, for this is your day. Dream your bright and happy dreams, and aspire to your lofty heights. I should be a pessimist indeed if I saw evil in the radiant dreams and fair hopes that now brighten your skies and make your path light.

But girlhood is not without danger. The rose may be blighted and never come to perfection, even though the bud burst open with the fairest promise, and the girl with the brightest prospects and hopes of womanhood may fail to reach her goal if she is touched with the blighting force of sin. Her God-given inheritance is a pure and beautiful maturity full of usefulness; but there is that which would ruthlessly rob her of it. We guard our bud-laden rose vines lest they be trampled upon, and we guard our precious daughters lest they be robbed of that untouched purity which is their own.

Girlhood is the time of making ready. Maturity and independence come later. For another period our girl must yet be under teachers and guardians who carry the burden and responsibility which would ill fit her young shoulders. In a few short years, oh! so few, these guardians and burden-lifters will all be taken away, and your girl will step into life's harness and feel the care and pain that have been the lot of womanhood since the beginning. So laugh and play and rejoice in your youth, dream your glorious daydreams, sip the honey and nectar from every passing hour. But guard well your feet that they do not slip into one of the snares and pitfalls along the way. Be pure, be true, be sincere, be earnest, and life will bring you peace and happiness.

Chapter Two

FROM THE CHILD TO THE WOMAN

Who can find a virtuous woman?
for her price is far above rubies.

One day I had a great surprise. I had been watching a young girl grow through, what had been for her, awkward, changing years. She was not pretty, nor was she very attractive, but she had a good, true heart hidden away under her blundering ways, and I loved her. I had not seen her for a few months, so one day I purposed to call upon the family and learn how they were prospering. It was a pleasant spring morning which I chose for this walk, and I tapped lightly on the door. Her mother opened for me and pressed me to stay with them for dinner. While we talked, I heard the sewing machine humming in another room, and presently her mother said, "Clara is doing the spring sewing for the children." I was surprised to hear that, for I thought of Clara as a girl too unskilled to undertake such a task. But my surprise gave place to wonder when a little later the door opened and Clara came in to greet me. It was Clara's voice and face indeed, but otherwise I should never have recognized my little friend in this graceful young woman before me. How such a change could have taken place in the few short months of my absence I could not understand. My little Clara had blossomed into a young woman.

Childhood is a wonderful thing. The little baby in its mother's arms, a tender plant dependent upon mother for all things, holds in its little body, not only the possibility, but the sure promise of manhood or womanhood. The infant mind now so imperfect and undeveloped possesses powers of growth and development that may sometimes make it one of the foremost persons of the world. Every name, though ever so great, and every record, though ever so inspiring, can be traced back to an infant's crib. Even our Savior was once a babe wrapped in swaddling clothes and laid in a manger.

Childhood holds untold possibilities and promises. While it is true that many men never reach their childhood's promise, never become noble characters, but remain mediocre and dull, it is not always because there was in them no possibility of better things. We must admit that circumstances and environments, as well as heredity, have much to do with the nature and development of children, but much more depends upon their individual disposition and effort. God meant that every child should grow into a noble, upright person, and there is in every child that which may be brought to the fullness of manhood or womanhood. Those who fail to be such have somewhere along the way wasted that which God had given them.

Womanhood is a wonderful thing. In womankind we find the mothers of the race. There is no man so great, nor none sunk so low, but once he lay a helpless, innocent babe in a woman's arms and was dependent upon her love and care for his existence. It is woman who rocks the cradle of the world and holds the first affections of mankind. She possesses a power beyond that of a king on his throne. There was the ancient Jochebed who received the infant Moses from the hand of Pharaoh's daughter, and in a few short years she had him taught so to love his people and the God of his people that when he came to man's estate, he chose rather to suffer affliction with the people of God than to enjoy the honor of being the grandson of the king. Womanhood stands for all that is pure and clean and noble. She who does not make the world better for having lived in it has failed to be all that a woman should be.

Childhood holds its promises, womanhood its fulfillments, and youth, those golden days of girlhood, the transition. This change is almost too great for us to comprehend. We marvel when we see the tiny, green bud develop into a mature rose of brilliant hue; how much more wonderful is the change from the crudeness and imperfections of childhood to the beauty and grace of young womanhood! We see this miracle performed before us continually, yet we never cease to wonder at the sweetness, charm, and beauty of every woman newly budded forth.

Wonderful changes take place in the body of a girl in this transition. She takes on a new form and new symmetry. Organs that have been dormant during childhood suddenly wake into life and activity. She becomes, not merely a person, but a woman. And with this change in her physical being comes just as wonderful changes in her nature. She has new emotions, new thoughts, and new aspirations. She has a new view of life and takes a new course of action. It is as if she were in another world, so completely does she change.

The awakening comes suddenly. Not that she will know the day or the week when the change comes, nor will she be conscious of the miracle in her nature, but the things of childhood will slip away from her. The little girl loses interest in her play world. She who did play whole days with her dolls now leaves them in their little beds whole weeks at a time. And one day she will say, "Mother, I do not play with these dolls anymore, and I have a mind to put them away, for they take up so much room." Then Marguerite and Rosemary and Hilda May are dressed nicely and, with a last loving pat, are tucked away in a box or old trunk in the attic and left to themselves while their little mother is hurrying away to the land of "grown-ups." Mother looks on with dismay as she sees these changes, for she knows that her little girl is getting away from her and that she must make room in her heart and life for the young woman developing before her eyes. She would put it off a little longer, for she will miss her little daughter, her baby girl, but even mother love cannot stay the hand of time.

Youth cannot stand monotony. So rapid are the changes in those eventful years that nature has tuned the mind and spirit of youth to seek and desire change and variety. Even a few days of sameness become wearisome to the girl. The more full life is of excitement and change, the more happy she is. Life to her is a succession of glad surprises.

The child becomes a woman at last. She slipped into girlhood naturally, and just as naturally will she lay off girlish ways and settle into womanhood. Life will take on a more sober look, and she will see things more distinctly. Many of the admonitions and reproofs that she received in her girlhood and which seemed hard and unnecessary at the time will now appear in their true light, and she will thank her guardians who gave them. Her cheeks will glow with embarrassment when she thinks of some of her girlish escapades and become redder still when she thinks of some of the things she wanted to do but Mother would not permit. She will talk more quietly and laugh less boisterously. New feelings of responsibility will press in upon her. Life will look more earnest and serious than it used to do. She will wonder how she could ever have been so careless of consequences. Our child is now a woman, and her nature craves something more real and satisfying than the fleeting pleasures of youth.

You, my dear girls, are now in those busy, changing years. I can have no better wish and prayer for you than that you may arrive in due time into the glorious state of womanhood with hearts pure and hands clean. Good women are needed everywhere, and the call for them will never grow faint. There will always be responsible places in life to be filled by women who are true and noble. Their price is above rubies; that is, their worth is more than all the riches of this world.

CHAPTER THREE

KEEPING UP ACQUAINTANCE

Acquaint now thyself with him,
and be at peace: thereby good
shall come unto thee.

*D*id you ever have a friend with whom it was hard to keep acquainted? You parted on good terms and thought of her as a friend all the time, but when again you met you found that once more you must become acquainted. I have had such experiences and found them unsatisfactory. I would have a friend be a friend all the time.

Nellie confesses that she often cries herself to sleep because no one understands her, while Marie acknowledges that she sometimes gets very angry with her mother because she cannot make Mother understand what she wants.

It seems that everyone, even your mother, fails to comprehend the importance of the very things that to you seem the most momentous. It is especially grievous to you that your mother does not understand, when you used to think she knew and understood everything. She appears to be getting out of touch with young folks.

It may be a queer way of putting it, but your real trouble is that you and all around you are not acquainted. First, you are not acquainted with yourself. You change so fast that you are a stranger to yourself. You cannot keep up with your notions. You want a thing, and before your desire can be fully granted, you want something else. It seems to you that nobody really tries to please you, and you get restless and dissatisfied. You think that everyone is crossing you, when you are really crossing yourself.

Watch the changes in your body. The pink dress you liked for school so well last autumn was, when you got it out this spring, altogether too tight in the bosom and too large around the waist, while the skirt and sleeves were both too short. You looked almost comical in it, and you wonder why you ever liked it, for it is a dress you care nothing about now. The dress is just as it was, but you have changed. You are grown taller and have taken on a new form. Clothes to fit you must be cut by a different pattern than your clothes were ever cut by before.

You are changing just as fast in your likes and dislikes. Mother has been planning a special pleasure for you, possibly has begun your new dress. She explains what she is going to do and how she is going to do it, and when you have a chance to speak, you break her plans all to pieces. She has not pleased you at all, though Mother knows very well that what she intended to do was the very thing you wanted only a short while ago. She looks at you perplexed, and you are almost angry that she should have supposed you would have desired such a thing. Perhaps you speak saucily, and Mother reproves you sharply and calls you an ungrateful girl. You go away and cry real, hot tears because you are so misunderstood. You, my dear, have changed and do not know it. It is not Mother, but the girl who lives in your body that so misunderstands you.

When I was about fourteen Mother was making me a new dress, and I wanted the sleeves made very full at the hand and open from the elbow down. They were very ugly and very unhandy and always falling into everything, and it was winter and very cold, but I wanted my sleeves made that way no matter what was said to me. Mother set her lips together and said, "Well, you shall have them." Her look called me to my senses, and I began to back down, but she said, "No, you shall have them just as you want them," and I had to drag and dribble those sleeves around till the dress was worn out. I found out that it was just a notion, which lasted but a short while, that I wanted such sleeves and that my real self despised them. Mother knew that all the time. I am not blaming girls for being changeable, but I want them to see that they *are* changing and not to expect everyone to change with them.

Again the girl finds herself feeling very awkward. It seems to her that she is always splashing or spilling something and bringing down upon her head admonitions that nettle her. The fact is that her arms and hands have grown so fast that she cannot measure the length they will reach nor the force with which they will seize a thing. She has failed to keep acquainted with her own body. She need not be discouraged if she has trouble with awkwardness, for everyone who is growing fast has the same experience. Father himself would be just as awkward if he were suddenly to gain a few inches in height.

It is hard for even a mother to keep acquainted with growing children. While she may misunderstand to some extent the present whim or fancy of the boy and girl, she does understand conditions much better than they do and can see when their desires and impulses would lead them into wrong. A girl is not able "to be her own boss" until she has passed these changing years. Not till then can she look upon things with a settled gaze. It would be very hard to judge a garden if one went by it on a run, and it is just as hard to judge as to what is best as long as these swift changing years are on. If the girl can only be patient and obedient until she gets fully acquainted with herself, she will save both her own heart and her dear parents many hours of trial and anxiety.

Strive to keep acquainted with your parents and teachers so that you can understand their point of view. Look at things from their side. Because they do not agree with you, do not go off pouting and keep to yourself, but listen and really try to see. I could not keep acquainted with anyone if I never sought her company or if when I was with her always insisted on having my way. And you cannot keep acquainted with Mother if you are always contending for your own way. When you contend with anyone you come up against their most unlikable side, and if you are continually contending with Mother about this and that, you will find yourself thinking only of her most unkind ways. Just a little of the deference and courtesy given to strangers would help you to better understand your mother.

Mother has many things to think about, and her mind is often full of perplexing problems which you know nothing about. It may be that just at the time when you are most persistent about something or other your contention is the last straw which wears her out, and she answers you more sternly than you think she ought. You feel abused and hampered. You think of Mother as being unkind and possibly unjust. She thinks of you as being stubborn and ungrateful. Both of you would see things differently if you took time to keep acquainted.

Keep acquainted with Father also. Too often he is not counted into his daughter's life at all other than to provide the money she needs. He is a great blessing in the girl's life if she will only give him a chance to know her.

He is busy and can hardly be expected to take the initiative in a hearty acquaintance, but he will appreciate the kind advances of his young daughter if she comes to him smiling and seeking to know him.

To keep acquainted with herself or her parents a girl must be considerate and thoughtful. She cannot give way to every fancy or whim, but must consider what is best for her and for others.

When a girl is just entering her teens she must watch carefully indeed if she keeps from being selfish. So much is happening in her life just then, such great changes taking place, that she is almost certain to become self-centered and to think always of herself first. It is such a task for her to keep up with her thoughts and feelings and desires that everybody else is forgotten. There is something about the tumultuous condition of her nature that makes her see with crooked eyes, so that things are not in their right proportions. Just a little reasoning on her part will help her to see that she is making a mistake.

It is selfishness that would make a girl think it a cross to help with the ironing because it might hurt her pretty hands, when her mother has to work hard all day long. Or, again, it is selfishness that would cause her to spend a whole hour dressing her hair in the morning before she is off to school, leaving her no time to help with the dishes. And when evening comes and someone must stay with the little ones while the rest go out, she has selfishness if she feels abused when her turn comes.

It is selfishness that makes a girl think that she ought to have better clothes than her mother has or that would have her want better than her brothers and sisters possess. She has kept her mind so full of her own desires that she has forgotten that others have wants or rights. It is the most cruel kind of selfishness that will cause a girl to speak crossly and saucily to her parents when they must refuse her some of her notions. They who have done most for her of all the world, who are working week in and week out for her happiness, who are denying themselves many pleasures that her life may be more full, they who because in their wisdom see that she should be denied— they must have her become cross with them!

The great foe of these years is selfishness, and the girl who comes to the most perfect womanhood learns soon to fight it with all her might.

CHAPTER FOUR

CHARACTER BUILDING

Let every man take heed how he buildeth.

The most precious earthly treasure a girl can have is a good character. Her character is what she really is. If she will look beyond what she appears to be and what people think of her, and look at her heart fairly and honestly, judging herself by the standards of right and wrong to which her own conscience gives sanction, then she can know whether she has a good character. When a girl is misunderstood and misjudged, it is comforting to know that deep in her heart she has been true, but it will rob even her friend's praises of the real pleasure if in her heart she knows she has been untrue.

Character is not given to us; we build it ourselves. Others may furnish the material, may set before us the right standards and ideals, may give us reproof and correction, may guide our actions and mold our thoughts—but after all we build our own character. It is we, our-selves, who take of the influence about us, copy the ideals, reach the standards, and make us what we are.

Youth is the building time. From infancy throughout childhood, material has been brought together which we may use in our building. There are home influences and teach-ings, moral and intellectual instructions received in school, religious precepts and coun-sels of church and Sunday school, the moral standards of our childhood's playmates, the characters of the men and women we know, and countless other avenues by which instruc-tion has come to us bringing material which we may use in our building. The girl who has been reared in a Christian home and by careful, watchful parents has a far better opportunity to build a good character than she whose life has been less guarded. It is in the days of youth that this assembled material is built into character. The nature is then pliable, and habits are more easily formed and much more easily broken than in later years. Day by day the girl, whether conscious of what she is doing or not, is tak-ing of the material which she has about her and is putting it into her character. Truth or falsehood, honesty or deceit, love or hatred, honor or reproach, obedience or rebellion, good or bad, day by day the building is going on. Through her infancy and childhood her parents have been responsible for her conduct, but now, when she has reached these important years, their responsibility is lessening and hers is increasing. Sometimes girls who have been quite submissive and obedient through childhood become independent and rebellious at this period, building into their characters that which is a lifelong regret. But contrariwise, others who have been unruly as children now wake to their responsibility and begin laying into their building those things that are good, upright, honest, and noble. But more often she who has learned to obey in her childhood builds the better character.

Character building is a serious undertaking. You would never guess it by watching the foolish behavior of some girls. Sometimes I have wondered that to youth should be given the responsibility of laying the foundation of life's character just when the heart is the gayest and the thoughts the least settled, but if the responsibility came later, it would be at a time when the help of parents and teachers is not to be had. The builder would then have to work alone, while now she has many helpers. And since to youth is given such a serious undertaking, ought not our girl to take earnest thought to what she is doing, that no wrong material is placed in her building? Can she afford, for the sake of present fun and frolic, to place in her building that which will give her weakness all through her life?

Character building goes on every day. There is not a day that does not tell for good or bad; each sees another stone in the building, hewn straight and true, or all misshapen and crooked. If temptations have been resisted and obstacles overcome, if evil thoughts and feelings have been quenched and kind and noble thoughts encouraged in their place, then a stone has been hewn for victory and right; but if temptations have been yielded to and evil thoughts and feelings have been harbored and cultivated, if wrong motives have been allowed, then the stone is unfit for a good building. So as the days go by, the builder sorts out and uses of the material at hand that which is put into the character which shall be hers through life.

A pattern is needed. No dressmaker would undertake a garment without some idea of how it should look when finished. She must by some means form in her mind the picture of the dress as it is to be when it is done. Nor would she undertake a lady's cloak by a kimono pattern. She would ask for a perfect pattern to work by. A carpenter would not start a building until he first had a draft which made clear to his mind just how the finished edifice should look. More than that, he would ask for a perfect pattern of every part of the building so that he might have it correct all the way through. No character is built good and true if the builder has not in her mind a picture of the woman she wants to be. And the pattern for a good character must be chosen carefully. The carpenter will not undertake a pretty cottage from the print of a barn, nor can a girl build a good, true character if she patterns after those whose lives are not good and true. She who has an ideal character is first of all pure and true, then earnest and sincere, patient and gentle, and more ready to serve than be served. It is easier to build a bad than a good character. One can always go downhill with less difficulty than up and glide with the current than row against it, and it is easier to drift with the crowd than to stand for the right. The bad character grows without effort. Just to be careless and indifferent to consequences may be the cause of downfall in one who would like to be noble. They who fall have been weak, for good character is strong.

Choose well as the days go by. Build for all time, not just for present pleasure. What you are building will bring you praise and satisfaction all your life, or it will be your curse and disgrace. Keep your measuring rod at hand and use it without stint. Reject all that falls short, no matter how pleasant it may look. "Is it right?" "Would it be for my good?" "Does it meet the approval of my parents or teachers?" "Is it forbidden?" are questions which you should be continually asking yourself as you decide what to do and what to leave undone. Many things that are fun end in wrong, much that seems pleasurable after awhile comes to be evil, and everything like this should be rejected without hesitation. To do right will often cost a struggle, but it is always worth the effort. We dare not allow ourselves to be continually guided by what others do. Christ is our perfect pattern, and only those who form their lives after Him are building the best character. He is the one great pattern for us, His children.

CHAPTER FIVE

THE STRENGTH
OF OBEDIENCE

Behold, to obey is better than sacrifice,
and to hearken than the fat of rams.

Our Bible class had been studying the lives of ancient men of the Bible, and among them was a man called Saul, the king of Israel. When he was first king he was humble and obedient, but afterward he began doing what he knew was forbidden, choosing his own way rather than following the commandments of Jehovah. There came a time when he was commanded to destroy a wicked tribe of people, with all that they possessed. He went out to battle as he was commanded, but he saved alive the best of the sheep and the cattle and gave as an excuse for his disobedience that he intended to use them as a sacrifice to the

Lord. The fiery old prophet of the Lord, Samuel, stood before him with reproof and a message from his offended God and, when Saul had uttered his excuse, said, "To obey is better than sacrifice, and to hearken than the fat of rams." More than this, he told the disobedient king that for his disobedience he was rejected of God and should have his kingdom taken away from him.

The foundation of all perfect deportment is found in obedience. All the universe is under obedience. The stars move in their respective places, the sun and moon in their orbits, and the earth upon its yearly course around the sun, all acting according to one common law that guides them all. The seasons come and go, seedtime and harvest, cold and heat, day and night, all according to laws that are never broken. And if by chance one of these laws should be broken, all the great universe would become chaos. All that God has made He has placed under law, and all moves on in harmony and splendor. Mankind also was placed under law, but not in the absolute sense that governs the universe. He was made like God in that he could know good and evil and choose for himself. If he should choose that which is right he *should* bring to himself blessings and peace, but if he chose the evil, he should bring down upon his own head the results of that choice. From this law of reward no man may in the end find an escape. Of all that God made, man alone dared to be disobedient. He who could have brought most glory to God has from the beginning dishonored Him.

There are two kinds of obedience. In the first a weaker person is overcome by a stronger and compelled to obey by superior force. His will is not in the obedience, but rather against it. He will cease to be obedient when opportunity permits. This is the obedience that criminals give to law, slaves to their masters, and which many children give to their parents and teachers. It is the soil in which rebellion grows, and it is always dangerous. Its end is always unrestraint, turmoil, and anarchy.

True obedience begins in the heart. The person obeying gives sanction to the law acknowledging that it is right and obeys because he believes it to be his duty to do so. He needs no law, officer, nor master to compel him, for he is master of his own soul and demands of himself that which is right. Such a man is great indeed who is able to make himself obedient to God and right. When the lesson of self-government is learned, one of life's greatest victories is won.

The girl who comes to perfect womanhood must learn to be obedient. Her whole life must be governed, not by whim or pleasure, but by right and duty. Her first lessons of obedience are learned at home. She becomes aware that all things are not for her personal convenience and pleasure, but that she must do her part in service, restraint, and sacrifice, that home may be orderly and happy. Her parents give her many and various commands. Some of them seem hard and unnecessary. They interfere with her desires and plans, and the temptation to disregard them as far as possible is great. She feels hampered and bound and unable to carry out her designs. But she who is building good character takes heed to the commands given her, whether good or bad, and receives the admonitions and reproofs which come her way governing herself by them, because it is right that she do so.

This lesson of obedience in spite of the rebellion in the heart is not learned all at once. But every girl does not have the same hard battle with it. Here is one point where she who is blest with a humble and submissive nature has the advantage. She can do quite naturally what her willful and rebellious sister will have to struggle hard to accomplish. Many girls are like my little friend Betty. Betty was willful by nature, and obedience came hard. She had been exceptionally willful in a certain matter, and her father had reproved her sharply, cutting off privileges that Betty valued very much. She felt angry and rebellious against her father for the penalty that he had exacted and unburdened her heart to her mother in angry little bursts. Her mother answered, "We will not discuss Father now. You are angry and cannot think clearly. But you will confess that it is not impossible for you to obey to the letter all that he has required. What your rebellious nature needs, my daughter, is to be compelled to obey, and you are the one to do it. The commandment has been given you, and if you want to be victor, obey it exactly, for your own soul's good. It is the easiest way out of your difficulty and the best thing for your development." Betty had the good sense to see this, and though her heart did yet rebel, she said, "I shall do that." And she found the hardest part of her punishment was over when she had brought down her stubborn spirit.

Obedience is never outgrown. It is not merely a requirement of childhood but is just as necessary in later years. After a girl leaves the care of her parents and teachers she remains yet the servant of duty. In fact, the more she is thrown upon her own responsibility, the more loudly duty speaks to her, becoming either a tyrant exacting obedience from an unwilling heart or a good friend and guide leading on to right, just as the girl takes it.

There were long stretches in Betty's childhood and youth in which the girl did practically as she desired to do. She followed the dictates of her own free will. It is true that to do this she had to keep within the bounds of law and order, but she found that no bondage. Now, however, since duty beckons her, she is pressed on every side. There is scarcely any time she can call her own. She must do her duty or lose her own self-respect. She has duty to herself, to her family, to her friends, to the church, to her community, and to her God. If she has not learned obedience and rebels at service, she will find her life hard indeed, but if she wills to do her duty and obeys from choice the commands of her stern mistress, then she will be happy in just doing her duty.

There is rare pleasure in obedience. The answer of a good conscience brings into the heart a peace and satisfaction that nothing can destroy. The girl who can fold her hands at night with the knowledge that throughout the day she has been obedient to God and right finds in life a gladness and quietness that nothing else can bring.

If you would be happy through life and make a success of the years which will be given to you, learn now in your girlhood to obey, to bring yourself under control, where reason rules, not mere whim or fancy. And the responsibility of this discipline dare not be left to parents and teachers. The girl who really learns obedience must take herself in hand and be a conqueror. Others can compel your servile obedience, but only you can bring to your heart true, God-fearing obedience. Only true obedience uplifts and enlightens and makes life noble. Be your own mistress bringing yourself into obedience.

CHAPTER SIX

MAKING HERSELF BEAUTIFUL

Favour is deceitful, and beauty is vain:
but a woman that feareth the LORD,
she shall be praised.

ometimes, much to my amusement, I read in the magazines those comical letters that girls write to the beauty specialists. If these letters could all be put together into one it would read something like this: "How am I to make myself pretty so that I shall be admired for my good looks? I want to be rid of all my blemishes, my freckles and pug nose and pimples and stringy hair. I would have my hands very white and shapely and tender, and I would be neither too fat nor too lean. Tell me, Miss Specialist, how to make myself beautiful." The wise man of old has answered this question in words that are most appropriate:

"Favour is deceitful, and beauty is vain: but a woman that feareth the LORD, she shall be praised."

Every girl is a lover of beauty. Beautiful homes, beautiful furnishings, beautiful flowers, beautiful fruits, beautiful faces—anything wherein beauty is found, there will be found girls to admire it. From the time her little hands can reach up and her baby lips can lisp the words, she is admiring "pretty things." And when a little of that beauty is her own, her pleasure is unbounded.

Every girl longs to be beautiful. There is in woman a nature, as deep as humanity, that compels her to strive for good looks. There is no more forlorn sorrow for a young girl than for her to be convinced that she is hopelessly ugly and undesirable. Oh, the bitter tears that have been shed over freckles or a rough and pimply skin! and the energy that has been expended in painting and powdering and frizzing and curling herself into beauty!

A desire to be beautiful is not unwomanly. A woman who is not beautiful cannot properly fill her place. But, mark you, true beauty is not of the face, but of the soul. There is a beauty so deep and lasting that it will shine out of the homeliest face and make it comely.

This is the beauty to be first sought and admired. It is a quality of the mind and heart and is manifested in word and deed. A happy heart, a smiling face, loving words and deeds, and a desire to be of service will make any girl beautiful.

A desire to be comely and good to look at is not to be utterly condemned. Beauty of face and form are not given to everyone, but when they are present, they may be a blessing if they are used rightly. But a girl need not feel that her life is blighted if she lacks these things. The proper care of her person and dress will make an otherwise homely girl good-looking. What is more disgusting than a slovenly, untidy woman! Her hair disheveled, her face and neck in need of soap and water, her dress in need of repair, her shoes half-laced, she presents a picture that indeed repels. Though she might have a kind heart and many other desirable qualities, yet her unkempt appearance hides them from view. But a person who always keeps herself tastefully and tidily dressed and her person clean and neat is attractive and pleasing. Her personal care only increases the charm of her personality. It is to be regretted if any girl lacks a feeling of concern and shame should she be caught in careless and untidy dress. She should take pleasure in keeping herself presentable and attractive, not only when she goes out or receives guests, but for the pleasure of the home folks as well. But when a girl paints and powders till she looks like an advertisement for cosmetics, she shows a foolish heart, which is not beautiful.

In the cloakroom of a certain school a question arose among some girls as to who had the most beautiful hands. The teacher listened to her girls thoughtfully. They compared hands and explained secrets of keeping them pretty. Nettie said that a girl could not keep perfect hands and wash dishes or sweep. Maude spoke of the evil effects of cold and wind and too much sunshine. Stella told of her favorite cold cream. Ethel spoke of proper manicuring. At last the teacher spoke.

"To my mind Jennie Higgins has the most beautiful hands of any girl in school," she said quietly.

"Jennie Higgins!" exclaimed Nettie in amazement, "why her hands are rough and red and look as if she took no care of them. I never thought of them as beautiful."

"I have seen those hands carrying dainty food to the sick and soothing the brow of the aged. She is her widowed mother's main help, and she it is who does the milking and carries the wood and water, yes, and washes dishes night and morning, that her mother may be saved the hard work. I have never known her to be too tired to speak kindly to her little sister and help her in her play. I have found those busy hands helping her brother with his kite. I tell you I think they are the most beautiful hands I have ever seen, for they are always busy helping somewhere."

This is the beauty for which every girl should strive, the beauty that comes from unselfishness and usefulness. Beauty of face and form is secondary in importance, though not to be despised. If used properly, personal beauty is a good gift, but if it turns a girl's head, it becomes a curse to her.

Think of such women as are much spoken of through the public press or who have achieved noble deeds, as Frances Willard, Florence Nightingale, or Edith Cavell, and consider whether you ever heard if they were pretty or not. No one ever thinks of such trifles when speaking of those who are great of soul. It is the pretty girl or woman whose chief attraction is in face or form. Those articles in magazines that so exalt the idea of personal beauty are pandering to the lower part of nature. One may be perfectly beautiful so far as that kind of beauty goes and lack to as great an extent that true beauty which is like a royal diadem upon the head. Those who give much time to increasing their personal charms are living on a lower level than is altogether becoming to womanhood. A beautiful soul shining out of a homely face is far more attractive than a beautiful face out of which looks a soul full of selfishness and coldness.

My little friend, be not careless of the good looks that nature has given to you, take care in dressing yourself and attending to personal neatness, that you may ever appear at your best; untidiness and carelessness hide the beauty of kind deeds—but greatness of soul and nobility of heart hide homeliness of face. You cannot see the one for the other. Seek goodness and purity first, then strive to keep the body in harmony with the beauty of the heart. Take time to make yourself presentable, but do not use the time before your glass that should be given to loving service. Let your chief charm be of heart and spirit, not of face and form. Seek the true beauty which lasts even into old age.

Solomon, in one of his wise sayings, expressed plainly the evil that comes to a woman who is beautiful of face but lacks the true beauty of soul. "As a jewel of gold in a swine's snout, so is a fair woman which is without discretion." As the swine would plunge the golden jewel into the filth and the mire as he dug in the dirt, so will a pretty woman who is not good drag her beauty down to the very lowest. There are many peculiar temptations to those who are only fair of face. Without true beauty of soul, a pretty face is a dangerous gift.

CHAPTER SEVEN

THAT MEMBER, THE TONGUE

*By thy words thou shalt be justified,
and by thy words thou shalt be condemned.*

That member, the tongue, what a treacherous thing it is! and how many times it brings its owner into trouble! One writer has said that he who is able to bridle the tongue is a perfect man and is able to govern the whole body. Solomon, the wise man of old, has said that "a word fitly spoken is like apples of gold in pictures of silver." A word fitly spoken, how good it is! It will heal a heart that is broken and turn away wrath. Kind words are like a fragrant odor that fills all the house. One person who habitually speaks kindly and considerately can soothe and quiet a household. And such words are not hard to give if the heart is in the right attitude. When one can feel and appreciate the joys and sorrows of others, the right words will come naturally. Unkind words are the fruits of selfishness. No one likes to be spoken to with harsh words, and if the golden rule is remembered and kept, none will be spoken to others. Consider the girl among your associates who is most universally liked, and you will find her to be a girl who sympathizes with others and who is ever ready to speak a kind and encouraging word. There is no amount of brilliancy that can, in the affections of our friends, take the place of kindness of speech.

A girl is known by her words. Generally the first impression she makes upon strangers is made by her speech. Some remark falls upon their ears, and they form an opinion of the speaker founded upon the nature of that remark. If she is heard speaking considerately and sympathetically, they think of her as kind and ladylike; but if she is loud and boisterous in her speech or if her remark is unkind and spiteful, they form the opposite opinion. Many girls have to overcome prejudice in the minds of others—prejudice which the girls have created against themselves by their own hasty speeches. It never pays to blurt out a harsh or unkind speech, no matter how pro-voking the occasion may be.

To avoid speaking unkindly at any time it is well to form habits of kindness. Betty had formed the habit of bidding mother good-bye each morning and noon as she set off for school. This good-bye was spoken in the kindest of tones and with a note of tenderness that cheered her mother all the day. One morning a stranger was present as Betty set off, and as she passed out the door she called back in her usual way, "Good-bye, Mother." Tears sprang to the stranger's eyes, and he said, "A girl like that is a treasure. You ought to be happy to have her speak so to you." Betty's little fare-well, said without a thought, had wonderfully impressed the man for good.

The tongue is an unruly member, and until it is brought into control by the girl her-self, it is ever liable to get her into trouble. If the old rule to "think twice before you speak once" can be remembered and obeyed, much trouble and heartaches can be avoided. When all the efforts at controlling a girl's tongue are made by parents and teachers instead of by the girl herself, it is like trying to stop a faucet by putting your hand over it. The pressure from within is so strong that ugly words will fly out in spite of their efforts. But when the girl undertakes the task herself, she is able to turn the pressure off so that the words flow smoothly. Not that it will be without a struggle, but victory is ahead for every girl who will try.

Every girl should form the habit of speaking in a gentle tone. While she is young the vocal organs can be trained to give out soft tones. Who is it who does not admire a soft and tender tone in a woman's voice? I have always felt sorry for older women who have from childhood spoken in a loud or harsh tone of voice, for it is practically impossible for them to do otherwise now. But girls can have gentle voices if they will.

No girl can afford to be impudent or saucy. One who is such sets a poor estimate upon herself. When a girl is saucy, she shows a lack of respect for her elders and superiors and also a lack of respect for her own good name. Instead of sauciness sounding smart and making a girl appear clever and independent, it shows her to be rude and egotistical. There is nothing lovely nor desirable about it, and if indulged in to any extent, it will spoil any girl.

Sauciness is more hateful because it begins at home. Where the girl should be her best she is her worst, for she is always more ugly to her own loved ones than to anyone else. She makes home miserable so far as her influence goes. Mother and Father may endeavor to be kind and just, but at the least reproof or counsel, the mouth of the girl sends out a stinging retort that hurts cruelly. Saucy words cost too much in heartache and tears. They are not found in beautiful girlhood, for where the habit of sauciness is found the beauty of girlhood is spoiled. Words can be like swords, cutting deep, not into the flesh but into the tender heart. The time will come, my young friend, when you will gaze upon the still form of one you loved, you will regret with tears and sighs the harsh words you have spoken. Do not lay up for yourself sorrow for that time.

The tongue, ungoverned, leads into many wrong channels. By it unkind remarks are made of absent ones, boasts and threats are uttered, evil suspicions spoken, trouble kindled, and hearts broken. Almost all the sorrow of the world can be traced back to the wrong use of the tongue. If you could learn the history of almost any neighborhood, you would find that someone has suffered, some heart has been wounded or broken, by the gossiping tongue of a neighbor. Gossip of a certain kind is not really wrong. We are naturally interested in the doings of our friends and like to talk their affairs over in a kind way. And it is one of the strongest curbs on evil doings to know that such will be soundly condemned by the neighbors. We should always be ready to condemn evil deeds. But when this gossip is mixed with a desire to wound or hurt another or when the one who is talking is careless of the results of her speeches, gossip becomes sinful and mean. When gossip becomes backbiting, it is one of the worst of sins. How quickly we would condemn a man who should shoot another in the back when only a short time before he had pretended to be a friend to him; and we despise a dog that nips our heels; and the girl who will talk about her acquaintances behind their backs and pretend friendship to their faces is just as mean. Any way we view it, evil speaking and backbiting are wrong and entirely unbecoming to beautiful girlhood.

The apostle James has written a few verses upon the evils into which the tongue can lead us, and we shall do well to read them at this time: "If any man offend not in word, the same is a perfect man, and able also to bridle the whole body. Behold, we put bits in the horses' mouths, that they may obey us; and we turn about their whole body. Behold also the ships, which though they be so great, and are driven of fierce winds, yet are they turned about with a very small helm, withersoever the governor listeth. Even so the tongue is a little member, and boasteth great things. Behold, how great a matter a little fire kindleth! And the tongue is a fire, a world of iniquity: so is the tongue among our members, that it defileth the whole body, and setteth on fire the course of nature; and it is set on fire of hell. For every kind of beasts, and of birds, and of serpents, and of things in the sea, is tamed, and hath been tamed of mankind: but the tongue can no man tame; it is an unruly evil, full of deadly poison. Therewith bless we God, even the Father; and therewith curse we men, which are made after the similitude of God. Out of the same mouth proceedeth blessing and cursing. My brethren, these things ought not so to be. Doth a fountain send forth at the same place sweet water and bitter? Can the fig-tree, my brethren, bear olive berries? either a vine, figs? so can no fountain both yield salt water and fresh. Who is a wise man and endued with knowledge among you? let him show out of a good conversation his works with meekness of wisdom" (James 3:2–13).

CHAPTER EIGHT

A SUNNY DISPOSITION

*A merry heart maketh a cheerful
countenance.*

*O*nce I looked upon the face of a dear little boy whose bright eyes and sunny smiles cheered my heart. I asked him what his name might be, and he answered, "Papa call me Sunshine John." Then I knew that the merry smile I saw was, as I thought, an index to the sunny little heart. Any home is blest if it has a sunshine maker.

Every girl owes it to herself and to her associates to be sunny. A happy girlhood is so beautiful that it cannot afford to be spoiled by needless frowns and pouts. There are clouds enough in life without making them out of temper. A girl who is full of smiles and sunshine is a fountain of joy to all who know her. The world has enough of tears and sorrow at best, and her sweet, smiling face can scatter untold clouds. Could a girl ask for a better calling than that of a joy maker for all about her?

Every girl must meet her share of bumps in life. If they do not come soon, they must come late. It is impossible that she should pass through life in the sunshine all the time. She must have her share of shadow. She cannot escape it. But it is not the deep shadows that generally cloud a girl's life and make her unhappy and sullen. It is the little things, insignificant in themselves, and which could have been passed by with hardly a thought if resisted one by one, that irritate the temper and mar the happiness. Every day our girl will meet with circumstances in which she has her choice between frowning and sending back a stinging retort or smiling and passing them by with a kind word. If she can pass these little bumps and keep sweet, then she has mastered the art of being sunny.

Betty comes in with a bucket of water and by some mischance knocks the bucket against the stand and spills some of the water on the floor. Mother is tired and has perhaps only just finished mopping, and she speaks up quickly, reproving Betty. "Betty, you careless girl, can you not do anything without making a muss?" Now is Betty's chance. She can frown and send back an angry rejoinder as she flounces out of the room, leaving her mother sorry for her own impatience and grieved at Betty's hatefulness; or Betty can look up with a smile and say, "Sorry, Mother, truly, that I was so awkward, but you will see that I can set it right." The smile that will come to Mother's face will be reward enough to Betty for her soft answer. Or, again, when the smaller children are cross and fretful, Betty can become cross also, scolding and threatening till she increases the uproar; or she can begin a romp or a story and turn their minds into new and pleasant channels. But before Betty can do this, she must have control of herself and a bit of sunshine in her heart.

If our girl can leave home every morning for her school or work with a song in her heart and a smile on her lips, and be ready with a bright "good morning" for each friend she meets, and an encouraging smile for the old or ill or those otherwise in need of encouragement, then she has found a sphere of usefulness that will make many people bless her.

There is a real art in smiling. Some people smile, or grin, all the time, and it becomes monotonous to those who look at them. These grinning people never seem to think who or what their smile is for. It is as if their mouths were made in that form. Other people have the kind of smile upon their faces that suggests sarcasm. But there are still others, and I have met girls who had mastered the art, whose smiles are tear chasers. There is something so understanding in their glance and smile that they make you feel that they care for you and want you to be happy. Sometimes when I have been discouraged or depressed by trials all my own, a bright, hopeful smile from someone has cheered me amazingly. In fact, we are very much dependent upon each other for courage and happiness. Then let us be dispensers of joy as we go through life, smiling and glad. If I am in trouble, having acted foolishly in something or other, then I do not appreciate the grinning smile. I would rather the face that looked into mine would express a little understanding and feeling for my trouble or that it would not notice my foolishness at all; when I find a friend who can meet me this way, then that friend becomes a real comfort and joy to me.

Smiles and gladness are like sweet peas in that the more you gather and give away, the more you have. Leave your sweet peas on the vines, and the flowers are soon gone, but gather them closely each day and they will blossom the more and last the summer through. So save your smiles for special occasions, when there are joys abroad, and you will pretty nearly run out of them altogether, but give them out at every opportunity, and the joy vines of your heart will thrive and grow.

Live in the sunshine. Look on the bright side, for always there is a bright side. No matter how a girl is situated in life, she can find something to be thankful for. If she is the daughter of a poor father, she is saved many of the temptations that come to the rich, and she has many opportunities for helping in burden-bearing at home. If she is a daughter of the rich, many opportunities for doing good are open that never come to the poor girl. Is she strong and well? She then has a heritage that can be used to good advantage in this busy world, but if she is weak and frail, her life can sweeten the shadows of home. Often the sick one is the most cheery of the family, in spite of her pain. Everyone can be a sunshine-bearer. God smiles on all who are willing to carry His smiles on to others.

In one home the daughter is a willing helper, ready to do all that her young hands can do to lighten the load, and she is a constant blessing to her mother, but she forgets to carry with her a cheery, sunny smile. Her heart becomes vexed and unpleasant, and her words sharp and cutting. The little ones watch Sister's face to see if she is cross. Mother's gentle voice often has to speak to her in soothing tones, "Daughter, I know you are tired, but do not make it unpleasant for the little ones. We have much to do, but love lightens it all the way." How often I have wished that to her other graces this dear girl would add sunshine.

The faces of our friends are like mirrors. We can look into them and see the expression of our own face. If we come to them smiling, we see a smile in return, but if we meet them with a frown, they will frown back at us. Try catching the eye of one who is looking sad and out of sorts and meeting her look with a smile, and see if it will not soon answer back in her face.

Especially when children are to be dealt with, it is necessary to learn to smile and be pleasant, for if you come to them cross, they will be cross in return. Be cheery, sunny, and happy both for your own good time and for the sake of others.

CHAPTER NINE

THE BEAUTY OF TRUTHFULNESS

Buy the truth, and sell it not.

A writer of old once said, "Speak ye every man the truth to his neighbour," and that is what I wish to say now. Once it was asked, "What is truth?" Truth is the foundation of all things, the rock upon which all things stable and dependable rest. When truth is gone, all that can be relied upon is gone. A life is worse than useless if it lacks the elements of truth.

Every noble, sincere person loves truth. For it he will give all that he possesses. Nothing is too precious to be given for truth; he so loves honor and uprightness that he would suffer the loss of all things, even his own life, rather than to perjure his soul. Men have faced imprisonment and death rather than swear falsely.

Truth beautifies the wearer. It sits like a royal diadem upon the head of all who possess it. Nothing so beautifies the face as a noble heart and a clear conscience. One whose motives are all pure and who has spoken the truth can look the world in the face without flinching. The light of honor and sincerity brightens the eye and clears the brow. Though the features may be irregular and the complexion imperfect, yet these beautiful qualities of the soul will cover all that and give to the homeliest face a beauty that is becoming. I would rather be known for the beauty of my character than the beauty of my face; would not you?

A lie is cowardly. After all that might be said to excuse an untruth, when you have sifted it down to its starting point, you will find its real reason for being is cowardice. Whether the lie was told to cover a fault or acted to pretend what was not true or said in spite and hatefulness, cowardice is the real cause of its existence.

The most common lie, and perhaps the least blamable, is the one told to cover a mistake or fault. This is done because the offender is afraid to meet the consequences of his deed. But a truly brave heart will not give in to this weakness. It is better to look up and tell the truth even if the confession will bring punishment and disgrace. It is better to be true in heart than to have merely the appearance of truth on the outside.

To be truthful, then, is courageous. Sometimes it takes more courage to tell the truth than to enter a battle. A young man once espoused a cause which was much spoken against but in which he believed with all his heart. In behalf of his cause, he stood before men high in authority, but it was hard to find one who would assist him. He especially wished to gain the favor of one certain man, and at last he stood in his private office for the interview which he had sought for so long. The man looked up at him sharply before he offered him a seat and asked him a certain question. Now, to answer this question exactly according to truth would without doubt, the young man thought, prejudice the older man before he had heard the cause. For one instant his mind was confused and a lie was ready to come from his lips, but he rallied and said to himself, "If my cause is just as I think it is, it is able to stand on truth," and looking the man in the eye, he told the truth exactly.

A look of relief came over the older man's

face, and he answered, "I have been interested in this matter for some time, but have been unable to find a man who would unflinchingly tell me the truth. I am convinced that you will do that and am willing to hear your cause." The young man was given a seat, and before he left the private office of the older man, a course of action was mapped out which in time brought success to his beloved project. Truthfulness does not always meet its reward so suddenly, but the reward will come.

The meanest kind of lie is one told deliberately to hurt another person. When the final judgment comes, such lies will be counted in with murder, for the same evil motive lies back of each. In the one, the perpetrator had the courage to strike the deathblow; but in the other, he was too cowardly to kill outright, so gave a wound in the back out of the dark. Would that such lies could be painted in their true colors.

The silliest lie is one acted out by a person pretending to be richer and finer than he is. You have seen such, I know. He is always seeking to be with the rich and distinguished, striving in every way possible to dress as well and appear as wealthy as the other. You will find girls of this class simpering and mincing along, scarcely recognizing acquaintances who are not well dressed, and lavishing much attention upon anyone well dressed and elegant. John, a young friend of mine, once gave a short, gruff laugh in his throat when I asked after the welfare of a certain girl, a mutual acquaintance of his and mine. I looked up, surprised at the way he had acted, and found an amused expression in his eyes and about his mouth, and he said, "Bess don't know me anymore when I have my overalls on. I have met her several times on the street when I have had to be out in my work clothes, and she did not recognize me at all. I met her the other day when I was dressed up and she was as friendly as ever. You know about how a fellow feels in the presence of such a person." Poor Bess, every right-thinking person would place the same construction upon her actions as John did. Those of real worth hate such double-facedness.

There is an adage which says, "Always speak the truth." But we should not construe this to mean that *all* the truth should always be spoken. There are many things which though true are far better unsaid. Unpleasant things will not help along by being told. It is far better to keep silence than, by speaking, to give offence.

Were I looking for a girl to fill a responsible position, almost my first question would be, "Is she truthful?" Though she might have the knowledge and ability, might make a good appearance and be ever so pleasing in manner, I would not consider her if her word could not be relied upon. A girl who will not always speak the truth places herself in a position to be continually mistrusted. Nothing will break confidence so quickly as an untruth, and it is hard to get back that which is lost when confidence is gone.

The best advice for any girl is to always speak the truth from the heart, to love and to keep it as her chief possession. So long as she knows in her own heart that she has been true, that she has not borne false witness nor spoken deceitfully, she can face the world courageously.

A bulwark of truth is absolutely necessary to solid worth. A character that lacks this foundation is weak and will in time be broken down no matter how high may be the aspirations and ideals of the girl. Practical, everyday truthfulness in little things and great things is the only safe course for a girl to pursue. Hold truth fast. Do not let it go. Be honest, be true, and let your words be spoken from the depth of a heart that is not filled with deception.

The really truthful person cannot carelessly break a promise. Her word is sacred, and when she has said that she will or will not do anything, she can be depended upon. I have heard mothers say of a daughter, "She promised me before she left that she would not go there, and I know she will keep her promise." Always I have thought, "Oh, happy mother! Your confidence speaks much for your daughter."

It is so easy to let a promise slip. First, it is given with little consideration. It may be that the girl is pressed to do something which she does not want to do or is not sure would be right for her to do, and, lacking the courage to say no, she promises lightly, never intending to keep her word. It is the easiest way out of her present perplexity, and she makes her fickle promise never thinking that she is laying a weak plank in her character.

Again, a girl in her thoughts makes a difference between people. There are certain persons with whom she would be very careful to keep her word and would be troubled indeed to be compelled to break a promise made to them, while with others she esteems her word lightly. Keeping faith should be held just as sacred with one as another. A promise to mother or little sister should be kept as strictly as if it were made to the most noted person of the city.

Promises whose breaking would inconvenience others should be strictly kept. If a girl has promised to meet someone at nine o'clock at a certain place, she should, if it is possible at all, be there exactly at nine. If she allows herself to think that quarter- or half-past nine will do just as well, she is actually stealing that much of the other person's time. That is both dishonest and untruthful.

Another kind of untruth often indulged in is the telling of falsehoods to little children to frighten them into obedience. This is very wrong because of the effect it has upon the character of the one who does it and upon the child who is thus fooled.

There is no angle of life in which truth is not preferable to prevarication. Too high an estimate cannot be set upon it, nor can it be loved with too great a love.

CHAPTER TEN

SINCERITY

*And this I pray, . . .that ye may
be sincere and without offence.*

To be sincere is to be in reality what one appears to be: not feigned; not assumed; genuine, real, and true. How much value we all place upon sincerity! What a low estimate we place upon the friendship of a person who proves not to be sincere, who, when to her advantage, snubs and ignores us. How we despise the actions of one who is lavish with expressions of love and kindness to our face, but who backbites us in our absence. We care nothing for her friendship, and her very expressions of affection are obnoxious. Is it not true that we expect and demand sincerity of our friends?

To be sincere is to be honest, honest with self and honest with others. Honesty costs something. To be truly honest is not always the easiest path. It is an easy matter to deceive ourselves and to make ourselves believe we are doing right when down in our hearts we know we are doing wrong. A man might give to a good cause and make himself believe he is doing right, when deep in his heart he must know he gives to gain praise of the people. A girl might make herself think she is studying because she is bent over a book, when she knows her thoughts are all upon the party to which she is going. A boy may make himself think he is smart and manly because he smokes, when deep down in his heart he knows he is being both disobedient and deceitful. There are indeed many ways for us to deceive ourselves. You have heard of the story of King Saul, how he saved alive the best of the sheep and the cattle of the Amalekites, which he had been commanded to utterly destroy. His excuse was that he wanted to make a sacrifice to God of them, when he knew all the time that he saved them to make himself rich. Many a man has built a church or endowed a hospital or school, or performed some other good act, to smother the feelings of regret and the fretting of a wounded conscience.

To be honest with self means to look things over with an unfeigned heart and to do right because it is right. When we do good that we might appear right in spite of deception in the heart, we deceive ourselves. When we least expect it, our true selves will show out, if we are trying this. Perhaps more people deceive themselves than are ever deceived by others. It pays to be honest with ourselves all the time.

It is just as necessary to be honest with others. Betty buttoned her coat carefully before she left her room, thinking her mother would notice what she had done and approve, for she had often been cautioned against going out in the cold with her coat unbuttoned. But that morning Betty had put on a waist that her mother did not wish her to wear to school, and that was her real reason for carefully buttoning her coat. She was both disobedient and dishonest. We sometimes think that honesty pertains only to money matters. It is true that we should always be honest to the last penny in all business dealings, but honesty also touches every other department of life. To copy or to take advantage in any other way at school in order to gain a grade is just as dishonest in its nature as to steal or to forge a note. The principle is the same, the difference being only in the magnitude of the deed. To take advantage of the teacher's back being turned to play pranks is also dishonest. To pretend friendship which one does not feel, to smile and approve to the face and laugh to the back, to be two-faced in anything, is mean and dishonest. Honesty or dishonesty is shown in every little act of life. It is the honest boy or girl who makes the honest citizen. They are the ones whose lives and influence amount to real good in the world's work.

To be sincere is to be hearty, that is, to enter into all we do with all our might. She who is sincere will give the best of herself to whatever work she undertakes. Even the humblest tasks become noble if they are performed heartily. It is a pleasure to watch a girl wash dishes or sweep a floor if she does it with a hearty goodwill. As for practicing music or studying a lesson, more will be accomplished in half the time if the work is undertaken heartily. The girl who does her work that way is a bit of sunshine in the home. God bless her! She is a comfort and joy every day of her life.

The sincere girl always makes a satisfactory worker wherever she is put. She does her work with a reasonable degree of rapidity and with a will as if she enjoyed it. Whether she works in an office, in the schoolroom, in the factory, or in the kitchen, whether her work brings her good pay or whether she is a busy home toiler who gets only her board and clothes, if she is sincere and willing, she will be a success. Her eye is not on the clock to see if her time is about up, but her whole attention is upon what she is doing. Sincere people are hearty in their friendships. Did you ever put your hand into the hand of a friend and have her grasp it with a hearty goodwill and look you in the face with a friendly greeting? Did it not do you good? It does others just as much good if you greet them heartily. Again, I have offered my hand to women who gave me tips of their fingers in a delicate, afraid-of-you manner that chilled all my ardor. I did not like it, and others will not like it if you meet them that way. The handshake is quite an index to people's hearts. Those who are hearty and sincere are not afraid to let you know it.

To be sincere is to be unfeigned—no pretension, no putting on. The girl who is sincere means every word she says when she is expressing love and friendship. I need not fear that she is only trying to make an impression on me, nor that she is getting my confidence only to ridicule me later. She is no turncoat and no traitor. It seems to me a girl can have no greater fault than feigning friendship and affection she does not feel. Those who are sincere are real. They are real friends, real students, real sisters, real Christians.

To be sincere is to be frank. Frankness helps a girl to speak right out from the heart what she thinks and feels. But there is a very unpleasant trait that sometimes passes as frankness. That is a disposition to say cutting things. There are many things that are better left unsaid. Even though circumstances have given ample room for severe criticism, it is better to keep the bitter word unsaid and to speak kindly. Frankness does not mean that we shall tell people what we think of them and their doings on all occasions. True frankness shows in clear, honest eyes and in a gaze of purity and truth, which brings confidence to all who see it. It will speak out of the eyes when the lips are silent. She who is frank keeps nothing back that changes the meaning of what she says.

Beautiful girlhood can hold no more attractive nor lovable trait than sincerity. When a girl can look with honest eyes and perfect sincerity into life and can meet the temptations that are sure to come with a heart sincerely set to do God's will, that girl will succeed. Her life will be a blessing to many. Old and young will be encouraged and strengthened by her presence and friendship.

CHAPTER ELEVEN

IDEALS

Strength and honour are her clothing.

What is your aim in life, or, rather, what would you have your life to be if you could have the choosing? What kind of life looks the best and most desirable to you? What are your ideals?

An ideal is a mental conception of perfection. It is a picture in the mind of things as we should like to have them. Every girl has her ideals and in one way or another is working toward them. She may be careless and hardly conscious of what she is doing, yet certainly she is following after her ideal. She has in her mind the picture of the woman she wants to be.

No girl can rise higher than her ideals. The ideal one has in mind is the limit of perfection to that person. It is impossible to attain to higher things than we strive for, and few, oh, so few, even reach their ideals. So it is imperative that a girl set before her good and pure ideals, that she set her mark high. It is better to aim at the impossible than to be content with the inferior.

Every girl is a woman in the making. Some time she will stand in a woman's place and take a woman's responsibilities. And now, while she is a girl, she is forming the character that shall be hers through womanhood. Her ideals are shaping her life.

What is an ideal woman? What kind of woman is most to be admired? Who among your acquaintances seems the most admirable to you? Consider her dress, her lifework, her manner of speech, her influence upon those about her. Think of her as a housewife and as a mother. Is your ideal woman loud-spoken, or is her voice pitched low and sweet? Does she criticize others quickly and sharply, or does she have always a good word for everybody? Is her dress quiet and becoming or "loud" and bold? Does she wear jewelry and ornaments upon her person, or is her adornment that of a meek and quiet spirit? Is she a society queen or a quiet homebody? Is she a teacher, a housewife, a business woman, or a woman of ease and pleasure? Is she an actress or a movie star? Is she pure and noble or light and frivolous? Whatever she is, you admire her, and deep in your heart you want to be like her.

Out of these many traits let us choose together the ideal woman. First, she must be pure and noble. Our truly ideal woman must not be one who is silly or frivolous, nor shall she be guilty of actions that appear vulgar or unwomanly. She must be sweet-voiced and gentle—how a loud, boisterous woman jars on our feelings! She must have always a kind word for all—I cannot think of an ideal woman as one who might unjustly criticize me to my back. Her clothing must be modest and becoming—how could our really ideal woman wear anything that would cause those looking on to jest and joke at her appearance! Her person must not be adorned with ornaments, but rather she must be known for the beauty of her character. Her face may be pretty or it may not be, that is of no importance at all. She must be a good housewife and a good mother. She must be loving, tenderhearted, and sympathetic. She must be the kind of woman to whom you would not be afraid to tell your troubles. She must be true-hearted and loyal in friendship, never breaking faith. She must be a Christian, serving God with all her heart. If every girl would set up such a pattern for her ideal, how different many lives would be! But girls are liable, if they are not guided carefully, to become blinded by the glitter and gloss of things that are not pure gold. The dressy, extravagant woman, the social queen, or the girl seen oftenest on the screen at the picture show, becomes brighter light than the noble woman whose lives are telling for good. You, my little friend, choose well, for she whom you choose becomes your pattern.

A right ideal is worth striving for. The best cannot be obtained without effort. Effort costs something. We do not drift to the best that is in us, but we gain the higher places by steep, hard climbing. Every girl has much within her to be overcome and much to be developed. If her ideals lie in gaining culture and education, then must come years of hard study and application. If her aspirations run out to music, drawing, painting, sculpture, these accomplishments are perfected only after years of hard work. Does she aspire to be a housewife and mother? Then she must learn those homely arts that are woman's part in homemaking. Perhaps this latter vocation takes more earnest application and persistent effort than any other, for home touches the life so closely everywhere. Does our girl aspire to be pure and noble? Then she must give up all that defiles and leave it out of her life.

It is not enough to have good ideals. There must be a careful and persistent effort to live up to them. To keep these ideals perfect often costs the sacrifice of other things that seem pleasant. Like the merchant of old who found a pearl of greatest price and sold all that he had to purchase it, so a girl to keep her ideals pure must be willing to give for that all else. And a girl will sacrifice much for her ideal, be it good or bad.

It is not enough simply to strive for a life morally pure and noble. That is good, but the truly ideal life is one lived for God. A life which does not in word and deed reflect the life and teachings of Christ fails that much in being ideal.

I never think of one who stands by her Christian ideals but what I remember a girl I knew years ago. She was a happy, blue-eyed girl with high ideals of morality and godliness and with a purpose to be true to these in all her conduct. She had kept company with a young man for some time, and they had become engaged to be married, and she gave him her whole heart's love. But he was not a Christian, and as their acquaintance became more intimate, he saw more and more her determination to be guided in everything by her pattern, Christ. He loved the things of this life and desired that their lives together should be gay and full of worldly pleasure, while he saw plainly that her mind ran to things spiritual. He thought it best for them to understand before marriage that their lives were not to be religious, but should be given to the things he loved. So one evening he told her plainly his position. Her blue eyes opened wide in astonishment that he should set before her such a choice; for he had said that if she was not willing to give up her religion, she must give him up. She was disappointed, for she had hoped to win him for the Lord. But her answer came firmly from her heart, "I will not give up my Lord for any man." This decision cost her his friendship and the fulfillment of all the hopes and plans they had built, but she had in her heart the consciousness of having stood by her convictions.

And you, too, must stand by your convictions at the cost of things you love. An ideal is worth little if it is not worth wholehearted, honest effort. Nothing is more pitiful than a woman whose mind admires purity and right, yet whose will is too weak to choose them and whose life is blighted by sin and mire about her. Be true, be noble, aim high, and God will give you strength to keep your ideals.

CHAPTER TWELVE

AMBITION

And if a man also strive for masteries,
yet is he not crowned,
except he strive lawfully.

*A*fter discussing Ideals it seems right that we should next consider her sister, Ambition. They are much alike, yet they are very different. Ideals are mental pictures, which, without the aid of ambition, and that stronger characteristic yet, purpose, would remain upon the walls of your mind until they faded away with age and would never change the course of your life. But ambition comes in the eager desire and strives to make these pictures come true in life. Ambition is the ever seeking that which is just ahead and out of reach. To her who is following after ambition, there is no stopping, no lying down, no being quiet, but she must pursue her dreams and force them to come true.

She sees no chance of failure if she strives.

We generally speak of ambition as eager desire for preferment, honor, or power. She who is ambitious desires the best for herself. She wishes to rise high, to accomplish things, to be useful, and to be a person of some account in the world. Stagnation and uselessness she abhors. There are two kinds of ambition. The one is right and just and a necessity to the growth and development of any person. Without right ambitions, life must be a failure. This ambition makes a girl want to bring out the best that is in her. She who is fired by these desires will work and labor and study that she may advance, may grow in learning and ability. She is not thinking particularly of outstripping others, but of going to the highest point possible for herself. She is able all the time to appreciate the efforts and successes of others and rejoices in their advancement. Such ambition can never be wrong. But the other ambition rises from a different motive. The desire is not so much for goodness and excellence in themselves, as for the honor and praise such excellence might bring. Such ambition is satisfied with that which is inferior if it only surpasses what others have. In fact, this ambition feeds only on the failure and discomfiture of others. She who possesses it wants to outshine for compeers, to rise higher, to be more in the limelights than the rest. This ambition will cause a girl to steal or even to sell her honor, that she might have means to clothe herself better than others. And they who are fired with this unholy ambition will not shrink from perjury and falsehood to put down one who is opposed to them or promises to outstrip them.

Every girl's ambitions run more freely in certain directions. She who lives on a lower level is ambitious to be pretty, witty, and attractive. She is busy trying to win the praise and flattery of her acquaintances, to be thought the most beautiful, the most attractive, the best dressed, the best liked, the most-sought-after girl of her set. And if she gains her goal and realizes the fullness of her ambitions, she has but a handful of husks for her reward.

Other ambitions rise to a higher level, and the girl moved by them seeks to have ability in some useful and remunerative occupation. She seeks to become an artist or musician, a businesswoman or teacher, or to be a good housewife and mother. These are all good, noble callings, and if followed after with honest ambition and purpose will bring usefulness and happiness into her life.

But the highest ambition asks that the life of our girl be given for the good of mankind, that she be of all the service possible and in the best possible manner. If this ambition is linked with a life wholly given to God, then all her life will be indeed worthwhile.

Now we come to unrequited ambitions. We look upon those things that have been desired and attempted but never attained or accomplished. If these disappointments could all be brought together into one great pile, the mountain would fill all the earth. Here is the girl who wanted to go to college but had to begin teaching school, the boy who wanted to be a doctor but was forced by circumstances to keep right on at the farmwork, the man who in youth desired to be a great traveler but who has never been out of his home state, the woman who wanted to be a great writer but whose hands are busy only with the cares of an unappreciative household. Few there are indeed who have been able to accomplish all they desired and whose ambitions have been realized in life.

But this picture is not all dark. Youth is so short, and lacks so much in experience, and is able to look only one way, and therefore is liable to mistakes. The ambitions may be running in directions that are practicably impossible of accomplishment or may be ambitions which, if realized, would not be the best for the individual. So it is well that over us a wise providence guides and directs, suiting to each one of us the path that is ours through life. It is only when ambition dies and we cease to care or try that our lives become useless.

Suppose the fire hidden away in the furnace should go out because it cannot realize its ambition of setting the mill on fire! Or suppose the mainspring of the watch should break because it cannot become the hands or face! Mill and watch would stop, for these hidden forces held so resolutely in check are what move them. And so the life that seems to be hampered and held back from doing what is in it to do may be the very one that is furnishing force for others to work upon. Let ambition burn; never give up; fight against the odds that are against you, and you will grow the stronger for what you have conquered.

I would have you ambitious so long as your ambitions are just and noble, but I would not have you rise by putting others down. If ambition should die in youth or if youth should lack ambition, the wheels of progress would stop, all the wisdom and knowledge of the world would grow dim and pass away, and man would sink to his lowest level. But so long as the eye of youth is fired with those inner flames of ambition and purpose, and there are fields of knowledge and understanding yet to be explored, that long will the world's work move on unhindered.

CHAPTER THIRTEEN

THE POWER OF PURPOSE

He. . .exhorted them all,
that with purpose of heart
they would cleave unto the Lord.

*M*uch depends upon the height of the aspirations to which the mind and heart go in girlhood. The dreams of doing or being that which is noble and great, of accomplishing much, are a spur to every girl. And would you, my dreamers, have your dreams come true? There are three things which in the life of any girl will make her a success. The first two we have already discussed, pure ideals and noble ambitions, and the third is a strong purpose.

It is almost impossible to estimate the power of purpose in life. Things thought out of reason have been accomplished through purpose. Kingdoms have been torn down and built again, heathen customs have been uprooted and the light of Christianity put in their places, men born under the bondage of hard and unfavorable circumstances have risen above their environments and been powers in the world, the mysteries of the earth and sky have been sought out and their power put to work for mankind, yes, every great and noble deed that has ever been done has had for its captain and soldiers men and women of strong purpose.

A purpose in life gives something to live for, something to work for, and something to hope for. If the purpose be for a good cause, then the evil that would hinder can be overcome and the good prevail. But without this strong purpose, the individual becomes but a creature of circumstances, a chip tossed by the waves of life.

The power of purpose is the power of love. No man can cleave to any purpose with all his heart unless he loves the cause for which he strives. He must so love that cause that to give it up would be like giving up his very life. I once read of a woman upon a lonely ranch in a foreign land. Her husband had to go away for a week or more, leaving her alone for that time with her little children. He had not been gone long before she was bitten by a poisonous serpent, and she knew that in a few hours, not more than eight, she must die. She remembered her children and that if they were to be kept safe she must in the time left her draw enough water and bake enough bread to supply them until their father returned, or he might find his family all dead. So she worked and prayed that day, sick, fainting, almost unconscious, but love set her purpose strong, and she struggled on. Night came, and her hours were nearly up. She put her babes to bed and wandered out of sight of the cabin to die, but with a determination to live as long as possible for her children's sake. And morning found her still alive, still walking, and her system beginning to clear from the poison. She lived to tell the story, a monument to the power of a loving purpose.

Those who have made a success in anything have done so because they set about the task with purpose. All the great machines that lighten the burden of labor in the fields and shops and factories are the result of the steady purpose of their inventors. No man or woman has become of note in any work or field of research but has worked on with steady purpose when circumstances were discouraging. They loved sincerely the cause for which they labored, and they gave it their attention in spite of all that came to hinder them.

And you, my little friend, can make your life successful if you set to it with the power of purpose. When you know what your chosen field is, where your lifework will be, and what you want your life to accomplish, set to with all your might and fight till the victory comes. But make your purpose worthy. It is a shame to waste the power and energy of purpose upon those things that are selfish and of little worth. Undertake great things, things that make one's life bigger and broader and that are a blessing to others. One writer has said that without a strong and noble purpose, a person is like the lizard, content to stay in the mud and mire and hardly looking up to higher places, but that strong purpose helps him to rise like the eagle out of the shadows of the valleys up to the sunlight on the mountaintops and to claim them as his own. Every life that has been a failure has been so because of the lack of purpose behind it. Success is not always counted by dollars, nor by worldly honors, but in the achievement of noble and unselfish purposes.

It is purpose in life that gives an individual decision and determination. Every one of us must meet hard things. Success does not come down upon us as rain out of heaven. If we are to have success, we must draw it ourselves out of the wells of life. And we may have in measure as we draw. If we are only half in earnest, and our purpose is only a desire, then when the sun comes down upon us burning and smothering us, and we feel tired from our efforts, we will give up. But if our desire becomes a steady purpose to be, then we will not mind the sun and the heat and our weariness but will work on with our purpose before us. We will keep a strong determination to succeed in what we have undertaken.

Success depends upon your purpose in life. I shall ask you again, What are you living for? What is your purpose in life? When I last talked with my friend Betty on this very subject, she folded her hands and laughed as she said, "I just live and have a good time. I really have no thoughts about these things." And there are myriads of girls just like her. But sometime she will awaken to her responsibility, for her mother is yet the one whose purpose and decision are the groundwork of success in Betty's life. Sometime all you girls with patient, firm, determined mothers will waken to see that they were not just trying to hamper your good times by their much overseeing of your affairs, but that they were holding to a wise and loving purpose to see you safely into womanhood. I think that mothers see the hardest times when the girls set with purpose of heart to have their own way in something foolish and wrong. When two strong purposes come together, the battle waxes hot. Do you wonder what sometimes makes mothers sigh? You have the reason right here.

"I will if I can" is a good-sounding motto and shows a kind of spirit, but "I can if I will, and I will" is the old fellow who gets things done. You have heard the little poem about the man who undertook to do a thing that could not be done and did it. You can almost see "the bit of a grin as he waded right in" and the look of relief and joy when he did it. Have a purpose and stay with it. Keep on going.

CHAPTER FOURTEEN

DREAMS

As a dream when one awaketh.

*D*o you have dreams? I do not mean dreams when you are asleep, but those glorious ones that come when you are awake, where you are accomplishing the things you like to do, always succeeding in all your undertakings. Dreams in which you taste the sweets of love and praise and beauty, where your upward way is lined with achievements and failures are never known.

What a foolish question for me to ask a girl! I might as well ask if you eat or sleep. You would be just as natural a girl without doing either as to live without dreaming. Dreams are as much a part of your youth as are your fair and sparkling eyes. It is impossible to think of a girl into whose life no bright dreams come. Such a life would be dark indeed.

Dreams have a large place in character building. In them the dreamer works out many problems and comes to decisions as to what is right and wrong in many changing circumstances. If a girl will watch her dreams, she may know what kind of creature she is. If her dreams are of social conquests, fine clothes, and a life of gaiety, that is what she is in her heart, though her life may be ever so humdrum, nor will she ever be happy till she gets these things she dreams of. She is fitting herself to be satisfied with nothing but that of which she dreams. Her nature is being shaped to fit that kind of life. And how little such a life brings in real happiness! After the best that it can give is all devoured, the heart is left as empty and hungry as before. Such dreams are so much wasted time.

Perhaps her dreams are of romance and love, and she builds great castles in the air around that time in her life when one shall come who looks upon her as the best and most to be desired of all earthly creatures. She clothes him in the richest of garments and calls for him in fine carriages, and he carries her to riches and luxury. She is all outside the plain life as she finds it. Her eyes are large and dreamy as she looks into the magical future to which she is coming. Such dreams are foolish and silly and never build up good, sound common sense. They unfit the girl for usefulness and make her unable to appreciate the good about her. She will pass by true love with a frown of disgust while she is waiting for her love dream to come true. Such dreaming is not only wasting time but is making soft and mushy the character.

Again, the girl's dreams are of the time when she shall have a true lover, a husband, a home, and children. She looks ahead in her dreams and sees how she wishes to be a true wife, a good mother, and to fill the place honorably. She, in her dreams, sees many of the very circumstances that have come up in the lives of men and women about her and works out these problems always with the thought of God and right. She never allows herself to dream of being other than a true woman, behaving in a womanly way. Such dreams, if not carried to excess where they fill time that should be given to present service, are true character builders. A girl should look ahead to what she expects in life and endeavor to fit herself to fill the place as it should be filled.

Yet again, a girl may allow her dreams to dwell upon things that are not pure, and she may sip of forbidden pleasures through her imaginations. It is possible for her to become vile in heart with a mind as foul as the lowest character on the street, and yet live apparently a pure life, just by unclean dreaming. Such a girl has all her guards down and will, when the temptation comes strong, fall into acts of sin as well as thoughts of sin. Such dreams are sinful in the extreme and cannot be found in the girlhood beautiful.

Other girls dream of success in business undertakings or in some other chosen field of work. They not only dream, but set to work to make those dreams come true. I will say that no girl has ever made a success at anything in which her dreams have not gone ahead to brighten the way before her. She has been able to dream dreams when the circumstances about her were all against their fulfillment. They have given her courage and strength by the way. Such dreams are always good.

And again, we find some girls who feel deep in their hearts a desire for usefulness in some special way in the world. They want to be nurses, or teachers, or missionaries, or gospel workers. Every dream of theirs is of the day when they may be at these things. And, true to their calling, they endeavor to make their lives bend toward those ends. Every glorious life lived unselfishly in toil on these chosen fields is the fruit of these dreams. Without the dream the girl would never have undergone the work and hardship of preparation and service. Would that every girl had some such dream to beckon her on.

Mary Slessor, the "White Queen of Okoyong," from childhood dreamed herself a missionary in Africa. It is my privilege to know personally women who have given a large portion of their lives to gospel and missionary work, and they tell me of their dreams, which became more than dreams.

Why do girls dream? Because all life is before them, and they cannot but anticipate the future that awaits them. Youth is the time for making ready, and why should a girl not try to get some idea of the thing for which she is making ready? She is like a person standing upon the shore watching his ship come in. What goes around him is of little account, all his riches lie out there in the deep in that slowly approaching ship. So the girl stands and looks forward. All that has been in her life, and all that is now, are only passing and of little weight; her riches and joys lie in the ship just ahead.

Dream, my little friend, dream. But guide your dreams lest they wander off into forbidden paths. And do not let your dreams consume time that should be given to present service. The girl who sits and dreams of the good things she is going to do while she lets her mother overwork for lack of her help now is making poor progress in the fulfillment of her dreams. The girl who dreams of the time when she, a woman, will be kind and gracious to all, one who is loved for her thoughtfulness and gentle ways and yet who gives place now to sharp words and impatience, is wasting her time. The only dreams that are worthwhile are those that can be, and are, worked out in practical, everyday life.

A girl will dream; she cannot help it. She may let her mind wander on, wasting the strength and power that might come from proper musings as the power of the waterfall is wasted till it is harnessed and put to work. The true character builder harnesses her dreams and makes them work for her, building up pure ideals and a strong purpose to make those dreams come true.

Dream, but let the dreams be of usefulness and service, of purity and truth. Look away to the mountain heights, and, after looking, climb, climb, climb. Make your dreams come true. You can do it, if they are the right kind. God bless the girl with dreams.

Chapter Fifteen

FRIENDSHIPS

A friend loveth at all times.

riendship is a wonderful thing. The love of friendship is often stronger than the love of brotherhood and sisterhood. There is a cord of tenderness and appreciation binding those who are friends which is lovely beyond words to express it. Every truehearted girl loves her friends with a devotion that beautifies her life and enlarges her heart. She who is unable to be true in friendship has little of value in her.

A friendship does not grow up spontaneously. It must have a good soil in which to take root, good seed from which to start, and care and cultivation in order to become its best. The good soil is sincerity and truth coupled with kindness and affection. The good seed is love and appreciation. And it must be watched closely that no weeds of jealousy or envy creep in, and the soil must be constantly stirred by kind acts, words of appreciation and affection, and mutual admiration. There dare be no selfish interests nor evil suspicions in true friendship. The smallest bit of mistrust will blight it like frost. Friendship is tender, but it is beautiful.

An old friend is more to be prized than a new one. The longer friendship stands, the stronger it becomes if it is the genuine kind. New friends spring up and fall away, but old friends cling to you through all. Hold fast your old friends and those who have been friends to your father before you. They have your interests at heart. They will judge kindly when new friends condemn.

A person is made better or worse by his friends. If they are well chosen and faithful, they build up and make strong the best that is in one, but if they are unwisely chosen, they drag down and destroy all that is pure within. For a man will be like his friends. Show me the friends of a girl, those whom she most appreciates, and I will tell you what kind of girl she is though I never see her. Good girls have friends who are pure, noble, sincere, and upright. Girls who are careless of their deportment and reputation have just the other kind.

You will find them seeking friends among those who are light-minded and vain. A girl cannot rise higher than the level of her friends. Either they will lift her up, or she will descend to their level.

A girl should have many friends, but only a very few intimate friends. There is an inner circle into which a girl with true womanly instinct cannot invite many. Her nature is such that she must have a confidant, one to whom she feels free to tell out her heart's deepest secrets, but she is foolish indeed who tries to be thus confidential with many. The safest girl is the one who makes her mother her most confidential friend.

Every girl wants to chum. A chum used in the right way is a good thing in any girl's life. But there is a chumminess that is detrimental in the extreme. When a chum comes into a girl's heart closer than any other person, and to that chum is told every little secret, not only of the teller, but of her family also, and into her ears is poured out every bit of gossip and slander the girl hears, that chum is a detriment. When two girls plan together against the laws and management of their homes, vowing undying fidelity to each other in their secrets, chums become a menace indeed.

But when two girls can be understanding friends, each able to go to the other for help and encouragement, and whose plans and lives are kept open for the inspection of interested mothers, such friendships are good.

Fickleness in friendship is a common girlish fault. Youth changes so fast that she who pleases for awhile soon becomes dull. For a few weeks or months the vials of love and devotion are poured out on the chosen chum, and then in a moment of misunderstanding, the cords are broken and in another day bound upon another friend. To the new friend are poured out all the secrets gained from the old friend, and so the gossip grows. A girl who will become "miffed" with her friend and tell what she has sacredly promised to keep is not worthy of being called a friend.

Some girls take their girlhood friendships too seriously. They allow a sentimental love to bind itself around a chum so that a *few* weeks of separation may cause "oceans of tears" to be shed. The red-eyed one goes about feeling herself a martyr to love, when she is only enjoying a foolish sentiment. In friendship be sensible.

When girls have friends among the men and boys, even more care should be used in their selection and treatment than when with girls. There is only a small margin between the love of friendship and romance, and what the girl may have begun only as friendship may develop into something more serious.

Again, if a girl will make herself too familiar in her friendships with the other sex, she is liable to give them a wrong conception of her. She may appear to them to be only a "good fellow," and they may interpret that appellation to mean that she has let down some of her womanly guards and does not expect to be treated with the deference and respect usually given to good women. Any girl is in a dangerous position when she gets this reputation.

Kitty Lane was an upright girl, but in her work in the office she fell into the way of joking freely with the men, and she took their jokes in as good a humor. They all seemed friendly enough with her and in a way seemed to appreciate her. It was not until she had begun to appreciate in a particular manner the attentions of a newcomer into their midst she found out what she had been doing. He suddenly stopped his attentions, and though he treated her with respect, he was cold toward her. At last she could endure the suspense no longer and went to him to know what had changed him so. He hesitated in telling her until she insisted very earnestly.

"Miss Lane, I meant my friendship just as any pure-minded man means the attentions such as I was giving you. But I overheard the conversations of some of the men and learned that you were known among them as a good fellow, and some of them even made slighting remarks to me about my friendship with you. Forgive me, but you have forced me to speak so plainly. I want my wife to come into my home with a record of womanliness and purity."

This was cruel indeed, and she protested her innocence to him. His answer again seemed just as cruel and was her reward for seeking and maintaining, in her free way, friendship with men. "Miss Lane, I believe you, but your conduct does not always give that appearance. The girl men will joke with is not the girl they wish to marry." He considered her guards too low for him to trust.

True friendship will never ask a woman to step down from her womanly dignity and discretion. She holds her honor and her appearance of honor higher than everything else.

My little friend, choose your friends carefully, and keep them loyally. While you are kind to those who have fallen, remember that it is not for you, a young girl, to raise them up by seeking their company. You are too easily drawn away yourself. Let your friends be from among those whom you consider your superiors, that is, those whose conversation and deportment will lead you up instead of down. If you are a young Christian, seek your friends among those who have been longer in the way. Keep out of the company of those who draw your mind away from things that are right.

Old friends of your parents who have proved themselves true in all circumstances in the past, respect and cherish also, though they may seem queer and out of fashion now. Those who have loved and advised your father and your mother will be all the more careful in advising you. Though they be plain people and little used to the things common to you, listen to them and use their advice as far as you can.

Be a true friend yourself. Never let it be said that in you was placed confidence that was not deserved. Be genuine, be earnest and kind and true.

"A man that hath friends must shew himself friendly."

CHAPTER SIXTEEN

AN ACCOMPLISHED GIRL

*She looketh well to the ways of her household,
and eateth not the bread of idleness.*

I read in the society column of a paper the praises of somebody's daughter in which she was referred to as an accomplished young woman, and the reason given for calling her by this high sounding term lay in the fact that she played well upon the piano, spoke three languages, was active in club work, etc. I could but smile as I read, for from my point of view these are not the accomplishments a girl needs the most. Such things are good in their place, and if a girl can gain them, she is fortunate, but the best accomplishments are in the reach of every energetic, enterprising girl.

First of all a girl should know how to keep house. She should not only know how a room should look after it is put in order, but she should, by actually doing it, know the work necessary in bringing that condition about. She should know how to make beds, sweep and dust, and other hard work necessary to keeping a house in order. It should not be below her dignity to know the use of the scrub brush and mop. Though she does not do the work regularly, she should know how and be able to fill the place when necessary.

The girl should be able to cook good, nourishing meals. It is not enough that she can make fudge and salad and cake. She should be able to cook vegetables and meats in an appetizing manner.

The girl should be able to launder her own clothes and do it nicely. The steam will not ruin her complexion, nor will her hands be spoiled by the process. And she will have a great deal more up of hard work if she occasionally feels the backache that comes from this kind of labor.

Our girl should know how to sew and to mend. It takes time and patience to learn these things, but it pays in the long run. There are few girls who have never come to a time when these things were necessary.

The girl may plead that she does not need to do this kind of work, that her father is able to hire it all done. That may be true; but it is also true that many girls who began life in just such an easy way have come to circumstances where help could not be hired. I shall never forget the discomfiture of one dear girl who had become quite accomplished on other lines but had not learned these homely arts and never began to learn them until she had two small children to care for also. Small help her music and other accomplishments were then. She needed just the things we have been talking about now.

Our accomplished girl should know how to take care of her own body, keeping it clean and in a healthy condition. All her learning will be of little service if she is sickly and weak.

Our girls should all learn some useful way of wage-earning, so that in case of necessity she will be able to make her own way. Such things happen in life, when the strongest bars are taken away and the girl all sheltered from danger and hardship is pushed out by the hand of fate, and if she is not able to do something that will bring her a livelihood, her lot is a sad one.

And every girl should have a business education or at least an understanding of common business methods. Many are the women who face the world in terror because they must do business and have no idea of how it is done.

These things I have been talking about constitute, it seems to me, a real foundation for true accomplishments, and all that a girl can learn over and above these is that much to her praise and credit. She should know how to entertain. According to her place in life she should be able to be hostess to her friends and those who come within her gates, and do it with ease and grace.

While many girls are entering lives of business, teaching, and other occupations that lead them out of the home, now as always a majority come in time to be housewives and mothers. And since this is the lifework of the many, ought not they all to learn to be accomplished in those things that they will need the most? It seems foolish to me to hear a woman spoken of as accomplished who is not a good housekeeper and cook, and able to make and mend her own clothes. These are old-fashioned, homely accomplishments, but what every girl will need the most.

CHAPTER SEVENTEEN

THE OILS OF LIFE

Mercy and truth preserve the king.

*T*he great engine upon the track might have every part complete, with fire in the box and steam in the boiler, but it will not go as it should unless it is well oiled. While perfect workmanship and fire and water are all necessary, the oil is needed also.

Just so it is with our lives. We may build high ideals and have lofty aspirations, may do many good deeds and be prepared for usefulness in many ways, but if there is not in our lives the oils that lubricate the machinery of life, we shall be unable to make progress. You have heard an old wagon go by whose wheels lacked oil, or you may have tried to use some machine whose oil-cups were empty, and you know the doleful sounds of the creaking parts and the friction and drag of the whole machine.

Unoiled lives are just the same. They run hard, with much complaining. You can tell them by their lamentations and murmurings and by the friction with which they do anything.

There is the oil of kindness, which should go down into the heart, and which, working out from there, will make the daily life go smoothly. In fact, this oil is of little use if it does not go down unto the heart, for any that is only put on the tongue or over some special act for the time being will soon wear off and leave the machine as creaky as before. But she who gets kindness down into her heart will find it working out in her words and actions until she becomes a constant blessing in the household.

One who has kindness of heart is able to look upon the failings of others with consideration and patience, for she remembers that she herself is not without fault. She who has this precious oil in her life is not saying cutting things and giving way to hard speeches, which wound and hurt her companions.

Another oil very good to put on with kindness is called politeness. Used alone it does not do thorough work because it does not reach every part. It will help in conduct toward those who are higher or of more apparent consequence, but the tongue and actions will be rough as ever toward the poor and old and weak. But politeness with kindness makes a very smooth and pleasant combination of oils. Only when politeness is used in this way will it show a genuine character.

Little courtesies help along very much in oiling life. "Thank you" and "If you please" are two short phrases that oil a request and make it smooth and pleasing to the one receiving it. "I beg your pardon" and "Please excuse me" are two more little polite remarks that make good lubricants.

To rise and give your seat to an older person, to show particular courtesy to the aged, to speak respectfully to and about the old and infirm are little things, but they make glad the hearts of the aged pilgrims through life and cause their faces to shine. It has been said that these little courtesies are like air-cushions, nothing in them, yet they still the jars of life immensely. Let us have plenty of them to help us over the bumps in life.

Kind thoughts are also a good oil to place on troubled waters. If one will, by God's help, always keep his thoughts of those about him kind and forgiving, no matter how trying things may be, then he can go along without friction. Every unkind word and act is the result of some unkind thought. And some of these thoughts bear fruit almost immediately. So long as I can keep a thought of kindness in my heart, I can treat my brother well.

Patience is another oil much needed in life's machinery. There is so much that tends to annoy and fret a girl, that goes crosswise to where she wants it to go, there are so many days that she has to spend doing things she does not keep well oiled with patience, she is liable to become cross and sharp spoken. When anyone in a home runs low with patience, it is keenly felt by all the rest. The expression of the countenance, the tone of the voice, the manner of speaking—all tell instantly that patience has run low. Every girl needs a good supply of this precious lubricant, which not only smoothes the rough places but gives to the life a fragrance that is very pleasant. She who is both kind and patient is always desirable.

Thoughtfulness and consideration are two more oils needed in any home. The members of a family live so closely together that when one member is rusty, it affects all the rest more or less. On the other hand, if the daughter of a family can keep always well oiled in tongue and spirit with kindness, thoughtfulness, and patience, her sunny, pleasant smile will drive the shadows away and bring the sunlight into the home.

When I find that I am getting sore and fretted with the annoyance of someone rubbing me the wrong way, I may know that my oil-cup is getting low, for when I have plenty of the oils of life, I can stand a great deal of rubbing without getting peevish. And again, if I find I am rubbing someone else till he or she is getting all worn, I had better look; it may be that I am rough and need to stop the friction of my own acts with more oil.

The place to go to get fresh supplies of these precious oils is at the throne of God. Every girl who will seek may have of Him all the grace she needs to keep her life running sweet and smooth in her home and in her school, or wherever she may be. Or if she must be with those who are full of friction and strife, she may, in spite of it all, be so covered with the precious gentle oils that the sweetness and smoothness of her life will have a quieting effect.

Chapter Eighteen

HOME LIFE

*Many daughters have done virtuously,
but thou excellest them all.*

Not every language has a word equivalent to the English word "home," but instead uses a word meaning about the same as "house." How much more the thought of home brings to our minds than merely the thought of the house in which we live! The beloved ones living there and our associations with each other, our hopes and fears and joys and sorrows, all mingle together in one place of rest and sweet communion—home.

Home is a little kingdom with rulers, laws, and subjects, each with a part to perform in order that life there shall be perfect. The form of government of the home is the oldest known on earth, the patriarchal. Here the father is the head, the lawgiver, and the judge.

He divides almost equally his authority with the mother, and they two, together, govern the little kingdom. This is the only form of government that is suitable for the family, for the children are too young and too inexperienced to make laws for themselves. Not only have the parents the full control of the family, but upon them rests the responsibility of the family's support and of their conduct. If they do not properly care for or control their children, they must suffer reproach and shame.

To be able to fit into the home life and submit to the home government is one of the most noble traits of beautiful girlhood. This is not always accomplished without a struggle on the girl's part, for when the years of fickle, changing youth are with a girl, she finds that something in her nature rebels against the restraint of home. She finds that in many instances she would take a different course from what her parents are taking, that what seems most needful to them and upon which they insist seems needless and superficial to her, while other things which she thinks are very necessary they call foolish and silly. She wants to do many things of which they do not approve and will not permit and require of her what is irksome and hard. She feels as if she were being pressed into a mold that does not fit, while her whole heart cries out for freedom to come and go and do as she pleases.

Some girls accept their own point of view as correct and contend and argue for their own way until all the beauty and peace of the home life is destroyed. This is a grievous mistake and one that can bring only sorrow and regret in its wake. Other girls despondently give up to their parent's way and develop no mind or character of their own. This, too, is a mistake, which weakens the nature of any girl. But other girls submit to their parents because it is right that they should do so, yet holding, weighing, and considering their own opinions, really trying to learn what is best. A girl who will do this will soon develop judgment and discretion that her parents will be glad to honor. I have in mind now a sweet girl of eighteen who for two years and more has not only helped to earn the family living, but has done practically all the buying and planning of the younger children's clothes. Her mother is not afraid to trust the care of the children to her when they go out, nor does she fear that her oldest daughter will misbehave when not in her presence. She does practically as she pleases because she has by thoughtful consideration developed judgment and wisdom sufficient to be given that liberty. How much of the happiness of this home rests at the door of this sweet girl we cannot say.

The young daughter in the home has it in her power to make home a sweet, comfortable place to live, where laughter and sunshine will cheer the cloudiest day, or she may turn all its pleasures to bitterness and bring sorrow and heartache. If she can submit to her parents' control, can be obedient, kind, and thoughtful, she is a constant comfort; but if she is always contending and arguing, speaking up in a saucy manner when she is crossed, or scolding and quarreling with the younger children, she makes home almost unbearable. If she has a separate set of manners for her own people from what she uses when with company, she is a constant disappointment. I never like the blank look that a mother's face takes when someone commends the gentle kindness of a daughter of this type. She does not wish to lower her daughter in her friend's estimation, nor can she heartily agree as to her daughter's kindness.

A girl should have her full share of responsibility in the home. She should go about her work willingly, not as if it were an irksome duty which she was ill-disposed to perform.

She should count herself one of the family, one of the children, having only equal rights and privileges with the rest.

A girl and her father should be good comrades. Too often this is not the case, but they live lives entirely apart from each other in interest and enjoyment. This is not always altogether the girl's fault, but it is a condition she can remedy to a great extent by a little thoughtful kindness. Father very often has been too busy to keep acquainted with his growing daughters and finds them rather out of his range. They seem as much strangers to him as are their young friends whom he meets in the home. He thinks they do not care to have him about and takes himself off to his room or chair or on the porch and leaves them to themselves. One girl who found herself thus a stranger to her father formed the habit of going to meet him each evening she could get off. She was either at the corner or, at least, at the door when he came, and when she could she was at his office that they might have the whole way home together. It was only a little while until homecoming was the happiest part of both their days, and many loving confidences were exchanged, which would never have been possible without her first step.

Another family had the "father's hour," as they called it, the first hour after supper, and both he and they planned their day to have this hour together. Fathers do like to be counted in.

Any girl who will speak disrespectfully either to or of her father is lacking in one of the first principles of real womanhood. She should always remember that Father has the right to direct her life, to say what she shall and shall not do, to forbid her to go anywhere that is not proper. His word to her should be final. His approval to her should mean much.

The daughter and her mother come into closer relationship. They touch each other on many more points than do daughter and father. And if the daughter is safe from the temptations and allurements of sin about her, she is a girl who makes her mother her chief confidant. To her goes every secret, every hope, and every fear. All the perplexities of her young life are threshed out by Mother's side.

But Mother has to look after so many departments of Daughter's life that her over-seeing becomes a trial to the girl. There is a certain portion of a girl's life when her mother has to be responsible for the way she arranges her hair, for the dress she wears and the way she gets it on, and for her whereabouts and who she is with practically every hour of the day. I do not mean that only in childhood does the girl need this oversight, but while she is in her teens also. Not until her judgment and discretion develop along with the wisdom and prudence can a girl be safely left to look out for herself. Because Mother is obliged to direct so much of Daughter's life, it sometimes happens that it appears to Daughter as if Mother met her on every hand with restraint, as if she gave her no liberty. Sometimes the relations between them become strained. This is hard for the mother and discouraging for the daughter. But Mother can hardly give up her responsibility so long as Daughter is not able to carry it properly herself. Now is the time for Daughter to submit, to wait, to look well to her ways. Only when her parents see that she can bear responsibility will they willingly give it to her.

One of the sweetest places a young girl may have in any home is that of big sister. What a field of happiness and usefulness is open to the girl with little brothers and sisters! They are ready to look up to her as a guide and a pattern in everything. If she manages rightly, she can have unlimited influence with them.

Have you seen her, the ideal big sister? She is ever ready to kiss away the bumps and bruises of little heads and hearts, she knows just how to mend broken dolls and balls, she likes to popcorn and make candy for little people to eat, she knows such wonderful stories to tell or read, she will pick up and put out of sight those evidences of childish neglect that might bring little people into trouble, she understands and is a companion for every one of them. Yes, many homes have just such older daughters as that.

The girl who is learning day by day to be a good daughter at home and a good sister to the younger children is also learning day by day how to make in time a good wife and a good mother. She is getting ready for the greatest work a woman can do. It was a woman who had given her life for a noble and far-reaching work, and who had never married, who when someone commended her for the much that she had accomplished, said, "I would give it all for a pair of baby hands." There is no work so good for any woman as making a good, true home for somebody. Every truly beautiful character is its best at home. Let us never neglect the home life.

CHAPTER NINETEEN

A CONVERSATION ON DRESS

Adorn themselves in modest apparel.

"Mother," said Jennie Vane one day as the two sat together sewing, "why do you not want me to wear my dress necks low?"

"What would you consider a low-necked dress?" asked her mother.

"You know how the girls wear them, low like this," said Jennie, with her finger making on her bosom a line that she called low. Mrs. Vane looked up to God for wisdom to rightly answer and to direct the conversation that some of the principles of dress might be planted deeply in Jennie's mind.

"I do not require you to make your dresses with close-fitting necks, Jennie, but I have reasons which I am only too glad to explain to you why I do not approve such necks as you have described."

"I want to know just why, Mother, for sometimes I feel a little queer that none of my dresses are made that way."

"One of the first requisites of a real lady is that she should be modest. By modesty we mean that she shall not say, do, nor wear anything that would cause her to appear 'loud,' vulgar, or unchaste. There should be nothing about her to attract unfavorable attention, nothing in her dress or manner that would give evil-minded men an excuse for vulgar comment. For many generations the good women of our country have believed that modesty requires them to wear clothing that covers their bodies and limbs. Wherever this rule has been broken, many blighted lives have been the cost. When we dress contrary to this rule we give excuse for evil thoughts in the minds of those who look upon us, and every girl who oversteps these bounds makes herself liable to misunderstanding and insult, though she may be innocent of any such intention."

"Cannot men learn to take care of their thoughts?" asked Jennie.

"There," replied her mother, "is the very question, put in a little different form, that

Cain gave to God about his brother. Yes, Jennie, to a great extent we are responsible for our brothers' thoughts. But I would not have you think that all men are so weak. There are strong, true, pure-minded men and boys to whom these weaknesses of women are not a temptation. But there are the weaker also, and for them we are partly responsible.

"Let us suppose that upon the street corner there stands a group of men and boys, among them being two boys whose minds are pure. You and another girl are dressed with very low necks, very thin waists, and your skirts quite short. The scantiness of your dress attracts attention to your person. You may behave as perfect ladies, but as you pass the corner your appearance causes the evil-minded to think and say vulgar things about you. The pure-minded boys hear, and their minds are defiled. You girls are as much to blame for what has happened as the impure man or boy who said the evil things."

"I never thought of it that way, Mother, never!" said Jennie looking up with a new understanding in her eyes.

"Your dress necks should be high and close-fitting enough that at no angle does your bosom show, and your sleeves and skirts should always be long enough so that there is no naked or startling appearances. Also the very thin clothes that are sometimes called dresses are not really modest. We see some on the streets that are no more than a pretense of covering the flesh."

"But, Mother, they wear nice undergarments with those kind of dresses," said Jennie quickly.

"Yes, Jennie, but does a really modest woman want to publicly display her undergarments? Is that a fair show of modesty?"

The two sewed on in silence for awhile, then Jennie spoke again. "Mother, I know many nice women who do not think as you do about dress. Many church members dress the very way you have been condemning. Do you think they are not nice women or are not Christians? I cannot think that."

"That is entirely another side of the question, Jennie. I must answer for myself before God, and so must they. But it remains a fact that many nice women dress in a way that is not strictly modest. Many do not think; they just do as the rest do. It is the same with some women who really love the Lord. Their minds and hearts are not awake on this line. They follow where the present fads lead with no thought of the consequences.

"I cannot say to you that nice women do not dress as I have been condemning, for you and I both know nice women often do. Nor can we say that Christians never wear such things, for we have seen examples where those who showed they were actually Christians did wear them. So we cannot look round at others for examples. We must have a conscience toward God ourselves and answer these questions before Him in our own hearts. As for myself I cannot wear what I know is not becomingly modest for a Christian to wear."

"But I am not a Christian. I have not been converted," suggested Jennie, as if she had now found an excuse.

"But you should be, Jennie. That does not change your responsibility before God. If it is not right for a Christian to do it, it is wrong for anyone to do it." Mrs. Vane sat still a little while, thinking, then continued. "It is not merely a matter of opinion, but of principle. Do startling clothes cause unfavorable attention and comment? Are they modest? Should modest women wear them? Am I discharging my duty as a Christian either to wear them or to permit my daughter to do so? Is my daughter safe with them on, from the insults of base men?"

"Of course, if you put it that way, Mother, it certainly looks as if wearing such things is wrong. But it seems queer to me that we should need to be so different from other people."

"That is all owing to the way you look, Jennie. If you will look in the right direction you will find many, many women and girls who are not overstepping the bounds of womanly modesty, and they do not look queer either."

"Is it for the same reason that you want me always to do my hair simply?" again asked Jennie.

"Partly. The manner of dressing the hair will give a girl a modest, or a bold, exaggerated look. And then, many of the extravagant headdresses are unbecoming to most faces. I cannot see why you should make yourself look outlandish by your headdress just because six out of every seven girls are doing it. It is far better to choose a mode of hair-dress that becomes your face and stick to it, than to be changing from one thing to another. Besides, we wish you to take good care of your hair that you may preserve its beauty."

"But, Mother, I like to do as the rest do. I hate to be different from other girls," persisted Jennie.

"Be frank with me, Jennie: Are you so different from others? Are there not many of your schoolgirl friends who dress just as modestly as you do? And are there not a number of girls yet who are not extravagant in their hairdressing? Be honest with me: Are there not many girls like you?"

"Oh, yes, for that matter. But they are not the ones we look at. Some of the girls have a new way of dressing their hair every week."

"But the quiet, sensible girls run a far greater chance of coming to pure, wholesome womanhood. Jennie, dear, sometime you will be thankful that you are one of them."

CHAPTER TWENTY

WHEN A GIRL GOES OUT

I have taught thee in the way of wisdom;
I have led thee in right paths.

I had gone out with Betty and Jean, two very dear young friends of mine, and we were comfortably settled in our places in the street-car when an exclamation from Betty made me look up. Coming into the car was a group of girls led by a pretty young creature yet in her teens. It was she who had called out the exclamation of my little friends. She greeted them cordially, and they introduced her to me as a schoolmate whom they had not met for nearly a year. While the girls talked, I could observe the new girl and her comrades. All of them had their cheeks painted too red, while their lips were a deeper crimson than ever nature made them. Their dress likewise was "loud" and rather startling, and their manner bold and daring. Tight skirts too short; low necks; high heels; extravagant puffs; giggles; simpers; hasty looks into pocket mirrors—in all showing themselves to be giddy, silly girls. As well as I knew Betty and Jean, I found myself wondering if I had been mistaken in them, and that if this was the type of girls they chose as friends, if in their hearts they were like this. But soon the conversation lagged, and I caught my girls watching me with furtive glances as if trying to fathom my thoughts.

When we stood again on the street the girls turned to me with flashing eyes and flushed cheeks and said almost in one breath, "I hope you do not think for one minute that we approve of those girls. We were glad to see Belle after such a long time, but she used to be just like we are. What has changed her so? Why, she looks and acts like a bad girl."

My mind was relieved as to Betty and Jean's ideals, but I could not refrain from pitying the girl who had brought upon herself their disapproval, and not only theirs, but that of every right-thinking person. No girl need hope to be classed among the purest and truest of women who appears on the street as Belle and her companions had appeared. A girl is generally taken at her face value; that is, she is thought to be just what she appears to be. Some people will take time to know her as she is, but the great majority in their minds pass judgment on appearances only. Nor are they far wrong in doing so. There are not many of us who can for any long time keep up a false appearance. Our real selves will show through.

The time was when girls did not go out on the street and in public places as they do now. In some Oriental countries yet the women are kept secluded, and shut away from the eyes of all but their own family. When the Western nations broke away from these old customs of seclusion, they yet kept their wives and daughters away from public life. But all that is changed now, and women and girls go upon the street and in public places as freely as do the men. This change in customs gives the girls many outlets for their energies and efforts that formerly were closed to them, but it also gives them many more temptations. You who are living through a beautiful girlhood want to know how to use these new opportunities and yet escape the temptations that they bring.

When a girl dresses to go on the street she

should prepare herself in becoming dress, being neither untidy nor conspicuous for the brightness and gaudiness of her clothes. She should remember that upon the street, she meets all kinds of people, and among them will be some who would put an evil construction upon any carelessness in this respect. It is for her protection and good name that we would insist upon a street dress that is modest and unassuming. The more simple the street dress the better it is. Also, her hair should be one in a simple manner and such as is becoming to her face and years. She should strive to look just what she is, a quiet, unassuming girl going about her own affairs.

The cheeks and lips painted a scarlet beyond anything nature would ever give is bad taste at any time, and is an index to a vain and foolish heart, and will not be found in beautiful girlhood. Good health and perfect cleanliness will bring a rosiness and flush to both cheek and lip that is far more beautiful than anything that can be rubbed on.

When the girl is on the street or in public places she should never laugh nor talk loudly. To do so will only call upon her undesirable attention and criticism, and it is a sign of vulgarity. A real lady will not do so. Neither will she be giggling and simpering, nor in any of her conduct will she seek to draw attention to herself. She will not act boisterous nor rowdy, nor keep the company of those who do so act. There will be something about her which is a reproof to those who would be boisterous.

A girl should never loiter about public places when she has no business calling her there. If she does so, she is forced into temptation and made an object of criticism, which will in time bring her into very undesirable situations. One girl, a very young girl, who had formed the habit of loitering about a depot at train time, picking up a conversation with some of the men she met there, thinking only of the fun there was in it, had the following experience:

One day a gentleman alighted from a train which was to wait for the passengers to eat. He began walking up and down the platform. He was fine-looking and soon attracted the attention of this girl. She watched him furtively out of the corner of her eye, coughed a little, and laughed merrily and a trifle loudly with a group of her acquaintances, but at first he paid no attention. This piqued her, and she made more ardent efforts to attract his attention, for her companions were teasing her at her failure to "land her catch." Her power of attraction was being tested.

At last he noticed, turned, and sought her out and came directly to her, while her foolish little heart was all in a flutter at her success. She meant to do no more than to chat with him a few moments, and by so doing satisfy her vanity as to her attractiveness, and clear herself of the charge of weakness the girls had teasingly made.

"My dear girl," he said, tipping his hat, "have you a mother at home?"

"Why, yes," the girl stammered.

"Then go to her and tell her to keep you with her until you learn how you ought to behave in a public place," and saying this he turned and left her in confusion and shame. It was a hard rebuke, but this man had told her only what every pure-minded man and woman was thinking. Girls can hardly afford to call down upon themselves such severe criticism.

A young man was walking down the street of a small city intent only upon his own affairs; but he happened to be good-looking, and a group of schoolgirls spied him, and one of them expressed her decision to make his acquaintance and find out who he was. She and her companions walked rapidly and overtook him, and passed him, laughing merrily and managing to catch his eye as they passed. Then they loitered till he had to pass them in getting to the corner, where he turned off on purpose to avoid them. They followed him and passed him again, and this time the girl who was leading the attack was more bold in catching his eye, and with a glance challenging him to speak.

He saw the challenge and flushed. He had sisters at home and had been taught by a good mother the proper respect for women. Stopping, he addressed her with a smile that was not merry, and she, thinking she was about to accomplish her foolish design, waited for him to speak. He said, "My young friend, you are not a bad girl, but you are acting like one. It is only a little way on the path you are going to where you will be what you pretend to be now. Promise me that you will never, as long as you live, do as you have done this evening, but that you will be a true woman." He waited a little for her to answer, turning his head so as not to see the painful flush on her face, for he was right, she was not a bad girl, just a silly one.

"I promise you," she said faintly, and he turned and passed on, and the group of

BEAUTIFUL GIRLHOOD

humbled girls hurried home.

If all men were as these two gentlemen, girls would not be in the danger that they are in from an unguarded act, but these were exceptions. While they set the girls back to right paths, too many would have led them on to lower depths.

There is no more beautiful adornment to womanly character than purity, and the girl does well to see that everything that concerns her dress and behavior when away from her home on the street or otherwise in the eyes of the public is pure, clean, modest, and quiet. Though she should have to pass by many things that other girls count good times, she will in the end be far happier.

Chapter Twenty-One

A NEW AWAKENING

*Remember now thy Creator
in the days of thy youth.*

Every girl who has had ordinary religious training knows that there rules a God over all who is all-powerful, and is called our heavenly Father. She also knows the story of Christ's life and death, why He came to earth to suffer and to die. She has heard and read of heaven and the angels, and our future home. She has also been taught that we owe our service to God, that we ought to do right and not evil all the days of our lives. She has been made to feel that when she does wrong it grieves God and brings His displeasure upon her. With many of a deeply impressionable nature has come a desire to profess Christ, and to serve Him fully, while they are yet but little girls.

But ordinarily the awakening to our need

of God does not come until the child has passed on into the teens. Some time in the early or middle teens comes a new awakening that brings the child into the presence of God Himself, as it were, there to begin answering to Him for its own actions. This change in the attitude to God is called accountability, and from that time on the child must answer to God for itself. Before this the child thought of right and wrong only as what was allowed or forbidden by the parents, but now he begins to answer to a higher court. It is in this sense a solemn time.

When a girl reaches the age of accountability, she has begun to feel a need of higher help in order always to have strength to do right. She looks with a new questioning upon the conduct of others, of even her parents, and sees in the lives of those about her a lack of true conduct or motive, and finds in herself an inability to do what she knows she should do, and the only help must come from One who is stronger and better than all.

This change of attitude toward God does not come instantly, but as the trees bud and leaf in the spring, every day bringing a gradual change until they stand in full leaf, so the girl week by week develops and gains knowledge and experience until she stands a woman grown before her God. At first there were only glimpses of character and purpose to which she wished to attain, now she understands fully what her duty is before God. And as she saw her duty clearer and clearer before God she realized more and more her shortcomings. Then came the natural cry of her heart for God, the longing of her soul for help from above.

The young heart thus first really awake to its needs finds the simple story of the cross and the power of Christ to save easily comprehended and embraced. The mind has not been filled with the doubts and questionings that often hinder those who are older, and the truths of religion are quickly grasped. This is the time when the greater portion of those who in later life become true, earnest Christians begin their service and feel the first touch of divine forgiveness.

The awakening of the conscience toward God is a wonderful thing. It brings a vague uneasiness that causes the young heart to stop and ponder and consider, and turns the thoughts naturally to holy things. If our girl will open her heart at this time, it is to ask of someone whom she trusts many questions about God and religion, and when she sits under the preaching of God's Word she feels a strong impulse to give her life to Him. This will appear to her to be her duty. She will feel a shame and remorse for the wrong she has done, and sorrow that she has not been a better girl. Compared with the new life she beholds in Christ and His love, she sees herself a sinner, lost and without hope of heaven. And when opportunity is given, she comes to God with her dear young life.

With many girls this first impulse to divine service is dulled, and she slips back into her old ways, but it is her privilege to go right on in the service of God, learning more and more of Him every day.

This awakening of the heart to its sins and the need of the forgiveness of God is called conviction. That causing conviction which whispers to the soul pointing out its needs is the voice of the Spirit of God, and she who hardens her heart and will not listen is shutting her door to Christ. He will come again and again, knocking louder and louder as her need is more clearly understood. But if she continues to reject the wooing of the Spirit, He will go away, leaving her heart harder than before.

When conviction is yielded to, it brings the girl to repentance. Anyone is sorry for

wrongdoing when caught or about to be pun-
ished, but the sorrow that brings repentance
comes because God has been grieved. And
true repentance will make a person quit his
evil ways, and make right his wrong life so far
as he is able. When a girl has wronged someone, or been deceitful or dishonest in anything, repentance will bring this all to her
mind and make her willing to ask forgiveness.
And repentance will also make her willing to
forgive others as she wants to be forgiven.
When she has done all that she can do in forsaking her sins, and calls earnestly on God, she
shall be forgiven, the Bible tells us. She will
know in her own heart that she is forgiven.
The Spirit who so faithfully warned her of her
sins and God's disapproval now whispers to
her heart that she is forgiven and is an adopted
child into the family of God. The burden of sin
and guilt will go away, and in its place will
come a feeling of peace and quietness.

From this time on our girl should seek to
do those things that are pleasing to God. She
will find it easier to do right, and will find a joy
in the service of God she never knew before.

This experience we have just been describ-
ing is in the Bible called "conversion," and
being "born again." To be converted means to

be changed from one thing to another. The converted man is changed from a sinner to a Christian, from being guilty to being innocent, from the wrong path to the right one. To be born again means to become a partaker of a new life. The one who is born again begins a new life in Christ. This experience is for every seeking heart.

Jesus said, "Ye must be born again." Every person who fails to come to Christ repenting and seeking forgiveness will at last fail to have a home in heaven. There is no way into the favor of God and the path that leads from earth to heaven but the way of the cross.

The Christian life is the only perfect life, and that can be attained only by coming to Christ forsaking the things of this world, which are contrary to His will, and following Him all the way. Beautiful girlhood must make room for Christ and the precious Word of God. There is beauty untold in God's service.

CHAPTER TWENTY-TWO

A CHRISTIAN

*The disciples were called
Christians first in Antioch.*

A disciple of Christ is one who takes Christ for an example and seeks to emulate and glorify Him in all things. Only those who are thus earnestly following Christ are worthy to be called Christians.

To be a Christian is the most honorable and righteous thing a person may be. There is no life, no matter how high or noble it may be, that can compare in satisfaction and happiness with the life of a real Christian. While the doors to many favored places are closed to the throngs, opening only for a favored few, this blessed life of Christian living is open and free for every one.

It was never meant that the years of any person should be filled up with the common rounds of life with nothing higher or nobler to lead on to greater things. The heart of man cannot be satisfied with the things that earth has to give. There was planted in man's heart from the beginning a desire to know and understand higher things, and to commune with his maker. The complete satisfying of this God-given nature cannot be had except by knowing God. A person may become very wise and fill his mind with many things, and put in all his time in learning, yet there remains something unsatisfied until he finds God.

Christian womanhood is the only perfect womanhood. If this is true, then we cannot find girlhood in all its beauty and perfection until it is a Christian girlhood. The life of a Christian is not too hard for a girl to live, if she has the right start and really tries.

First of all, to be a Christian, one must be born again. Christian living is not something that people put on whenever they get ready, but it is the result of the change that comes into the lives of those who have given their hearts to God.

A Christian girl is truthful at all times, is honest and sincere, is pure and noble, and everything that a right-living girl should be, but living that kind of upright life is not all there is to being a Christian. It is possible for a girl to be truthful, honest, sincere, pure, and noble without being a Christian. A Christian is that and more.

A Christian has taken Christ as her guide and example, and she will not refuse to confess His name wherever it will glorify Him for her to do so. She is not ashamed to tell her friends and associates that she is a servant of God. Though she may feel timid, it is not from a sense of shame, for she counts it an honor to be a servant of the Lord.

The Christian girl studies her Bible and seeks to make her life a reflection of its teachings. It is her guidebook, and by it she directs her path. If she finds that anything is forbidden or spoken against in that dear book, she lets that thing go, and she is just as ready to do all that it tells her to do.

When a girl is a Christian, she has learned where to go for strength and courage to do right. She knows the secret power of prayer, and is often found in her secret communions with God. Every girl has temptations to evil, thoughts will come that are not right, evil suggestions will present themselves, but if she has learned to go to God in prayer, she will have strength to resist every one and to keep her life clean. The more she has learned to look to God in prayer and trust the more beautiful is her life.

A Christian's life is not all sunshine and joy. The great pattern did not pass through life without hardness to endure, and so it must come to every Christian. One of the gospel writers has said that it is given unto us "to suffer for his sake." These sufferings must come but who would not be willing to bear a little for one we love?

There is something about a clean, positive Christian life that will make the girl different from other girls. She will not fit perfectly into all their plans. They will want to go to places and to do things that she feels in her heart it would not please her God to have her go or do, so of course she must refuse. They will talk in a way and allow their minds and thoughts to dwell on that which her inward consciousness tells her is not what she should do, and her quietness and lack of enjoyment in what they are discussing will rebuke them and they will feel somewhat uncomfortable in her presence. It cannot be any other way. The Christian girl will not fit in perfectly with girls who love only the things of this world.

And some of those with whom her

Christian spirit does not blend will speak evil of her, snub her, and seek to make her life hard. She will be persecuted for her life in many little ways. But for all that she may have to suffer from misunderstandings of this kind, God will supply grace and glory so that her life will be peaceful and happy anyway.

Being a Christian will not hinder a girl from becoming successful in any honorable work that she may choose to do. If she will remember that she is a Christian first of all, and never allow her youthful ambitions to rise above her desire to please God nor take the time that should be given in a peculiar sense to His service, then she may study and work as hard and rise as high as possible. It is only when her ambitions take the place of Christian purpose that they become a snare to her.

I have before now sat looking over congregations of young people whose faces were as fine and intelligent and whose hopes and ambitions rose as high as any you will find anywhere, yet whose countenances were fired with a light and purpose that was not of this world. It is a mistake to suppose that being a Christian will in any way interfere in those pursuits that are right and noble. If any calling will spoil the character of a Christian it will also spoil the character of a man. The Christian religion crowns all noble purpose and ideals and is a rebuke and barrier only to that which is impure and evil. The one whose girlhood is perfect may fearlessly say, "I am a Christian."

Our girls will meet some who live noble, upright lives, whose example of morality and generosity is perfect, yet who do not profess to be Christians, and who may even boast that they are as good without the help of Christ as the Christian is with Christ. Let us remember that such people are actually reflecting the teachings of Christ in their lives in spite of their boasts. They are as if the moon should boast of her light, saying, "See, I shine by myself. I need not the sun. This light that I give is all my own." We know that if the sun were not shining somewhere the moon would be without light, for she has no light of her own, she gives only what she reflects from the sun. The high standards of morality and generosity that these upright people boast about were learned from Christian teachings. Had they been reared where such teaching could not be had, they would be in as great heathen darkness as any people. It is foolish for any to boast of their own goodness.

The girl will find some also who say they are Christians, yet whose lives are not according to the Bible standard. She will find also that every other good thing is counterfeited—money, gold, jewels, everything of worth has its counterfeits, and so has Christianity. The thing that should most seriously interest every one of us is to see that we have the genuine religion of Christ, so that we may be rightly called Christians.

Chapter Twenty-Three

THE QUIET HOUR

*Commune with your own heart, . . .
and be still.*

Have you learned the value of a quiet hour? It may not be an hour literally, of sixty minutes, but it is a season away from the rush and whirl of the day, when you may get your bearings and know where you are. We live in an age when everyone is in a hurry, and the girl of our homes does not escape the rush. From morning till night, week in and week out, her hands are full of work and play. If she is an ordinarily energetic girl, practically every moment will be taken up with something to do, somewhere to go, or someone to see.

When we work too long or too hard our bodies become weary, when we think or study or read too much our minds become tired, and when things do not go right, and all our efforts will not pull them straight, our spirits get worn. For all these wearinesses the quiet hour is a blessed balm.

If the body is tired, to step aside to a quiet place and find a comfortable chair or couch to stretch out our weary body and let it relax to the very toes and fingertips, and there to lie till the tangled nerves straighten, resting, simply resting, will bring back vigor and strength again. There are some simple secrets in resting the body that are well to remember. To lie down a few moments upon the back with every part of the body possible touching the couch, just as an infant relaxes to rest, and remain but ten minutes will refresh the body more than half an hour or more sitting in a chair, or lying curled up on a couch or bed. Learn to relax if you would rest.

When the mind is tired, let the books or problems be put aside, and go to the quiet room, or, better still, into the great outdoors, and there think only of those things that are pleasant and in tune with the quiet and peaceful surroundings. Soon the thickness will disappear and the feeling of stupidity give place to clear, active thinking, and you will be rested.

But the quiet hour is best for the wearied spirit. The girl gets into this spirit-weary condition more often than some suppose. Plans are broken or frustrated, work that is unpleasant and entirely undesirable has to be done, misunderstandings come between her and her mother or others, she is reproved or actually scolded—oh, there are many things to set a girl crosswise with the world about her! And if a girl is trying to do right and is endeavoring to follow Christ in her daily life, she will look with alarm at the surging thoughts and feelings that seem set to overwhelm her. Possibly in the pressure of vexations she has spoken harshly or imprudently, and that adds to her agitation. It is now that a little season in quietness will do her good.

Let her get away from everyone if possible, and the door shut so that she is entirely alone, and then have a sober talk with herself. Let her rest her body a bit if she needs it, and quiet her thoughts. There will be something in the very quietness of the place that will soothe her ruffled spirits. As soon as she is quieted, let her pray and then think quietly and soberly. Though everything seems in a turmoil at first, soon it will begin to calm down with her own spirits, and order will come out of chaos.

A wise mother will, if possible, provide opportunities for her children to be alone so that each one will learn how to fall back upon himself for counsel and entertainment. If little people, when they get all worked up and out of humor, were more often sent away to think it out by themselves, many a hard time could be passed smoothly. But now that the girl has come to older years, let her learn to be wise and have her quiet hour.

Those who would keep their spirits in rest and quietness should not wait till driven to seek rest and quiet from every vexation of spirit, but should make a practice of going aside a portion of every day for meditation, contemplation, and prayer.

Prayer is more than the saying of words with the body in a certain position. It is talking with God, telling Him of your joys and hopes and desires, and receiving back His answer to your own heart making you know the things that please Him. To meditate is to dwell in thought on any subject. The Christian gains much by meditating on the will and Word of God. Prayer and meditation go hand in hand.

Let me describe a quiet hour of mine which shines out from my girlhood with brightness as I am now writing.

It was at the end of a busy day. I was never

strong, and the day's work had made me tired, and its perplexities and annoyances had harassed me, so that I came to my quiet hour with a spirit somewhat troubled.

I sat on the doorstep, with the clear, starlit heavens above me. As I looked up into the night my thoughts were something like this, "What a beautiful night! It is so calm and clear and quiet, and the stars shine so brightly. God, who is my Father, made those stars, and He made me. He is the creator of all things." Then I was lost in wonder as I thought of the greatness of His creations. I looked at the great distance to the nearest stars, and like a flash of light came the verse of Scripture, "As the heaven is high above the earth, so great is his mercy toward them that fear him." The thought almost overwhelmed me for a moment. I knew I feared the Lord, and so His mercy was as great toward me as the heavens were high above me! All that space was filled with God's love and mercy to me. My very soul seemed in awe at the thought. I felt so safe, so calm, so quiet and rested. Then together, my Lord and I, the day was reviewed. My thoughts went back to a place where I had spoken hastily, and I felt reproved and sorry for it, and said, "Lord, I will be more careful tomorrow." Then my thoughts went to a time at which I had kept still when someone had taunted me, and it seemed almost as by a voice, so clear did the assurance come to my heart, "I was pleased with you then," and I said, "Lord I will try to be even more humble the next time." So we went over the whole day.

I said (for the Lord seemed very near to me), "Lord, do I stand clear in Thy sight? Is everything right between Thee and me?" and the answer came back to my own heart in the quietness of the hour. "You are My child, and I am pleased with you."

It was time for our family worship, and I rose and went in, with my spirit rested and my soul as calm as the summer night. I have found that these quiet hours with God, these times when I have come as it were into His presence, have been the strength of my Christian life, and I know they are what every young Christian needs.

My dear girl, if you are not a true servant of God, the quiet hours in rest and pure meditation will make you better, and perhaps in them the precious Spirit of God will talk to your heart and show you how to come to Him. I pray that it may be so. But if you are serving God, do not miss these quiet hours with Him.

Have some time each day to go aside to meditate and pray. Be willing to do and live as you feel in your heart you should do and live after you have thus sat before Him.

Learn to love to be alone, to know how to depend upon yourself for entertainment, and to find in your own heart and mind something to think about and meditate upon. Do not allow yourself to be one of those light-minded creatures who must always have the stimulating effect of a companion to find enjoyment.

CHAPTER TWENTY-FOUR

MAKING FRIENDS OF BOOKS

Of making many books there is no end.

Who would not count it an honor to have among her friends the wisest, noblest, and best of the earth, and have their friendship so intimate that at any time she might go to them and converse with them and have their opinions upon the matters of importance? If only one such friend were yours or mine, should we not feel honored indeed, and would we not cultivate that friendship that if possible our lives might be brightened by the association? I am certain that each one of us would feel just such an interest in so exalted a friendship.

Would you be surprised if I should tell you that such a friendship is possible, not only with one or two superior persons, but with all the wisest and best of all time? That is the fact in the case. We are all provided with means by which we may become acquainted with those who have moved earth's masses most, whose lives have influenced most people for good, knowing the very motives and desires of their hearts and learning exactly what their opinions were or are. The medium for all this wonderful knowledge is the printed page. Through books we may, very intimately, know the wisest and best. I may take a book and go into the quietness of my room and there read, as a great personal letter, what the author has to say, and there compare his views with those of others and with my own, gathering wisdom for my personal store. What a privilege this is!

It is said that a person becomes like his friends. This is a very truthful saying, for association makes a great difference in the life of anyone. Especially is this true of the young. Boys and girls in the teens will almost certainly be like those with whom they most intimately associate, especially if they have chosen their associates. Like begets like, and we naturally seek out and enjoy those who are congenial to us, passing by those whose tastes and manners are offensive. It is not only the personal touch that makes this likeness, but the change of ideas. By the interchange of thought and expression all becomes to a great extent one, each giving to the other something of himself, and receiving to himself of the other.

What is true of personal friendships is also true of book friendships. If I choose only the books that I like to read, and after a while give you a list of those books, you can know, though you never see me face-to-face, just what kind of person I am, just how my thoughts run, and what I admire most in people and things. And if I habitually choose books that I believe will be the best for me, and read them carefully until I understand them and make their thoughts my own, I will in time become like those books in thought, and will be lifted out of the rut I naturally would have run in.

When a girl chooses her friends she should as much as possible select those who will be a help to her. If she chooses the quiet, modest, sincere, earnest girls for her friends, she will become like them; but if her friends are mostly the "loud," vulgar, thoughtless, and giddy kind, though she had been a reasonably sensible girl in the beginning, she will soon be as her companions.

So it is with books. If a girl will choose her books from those whose ideals are high and

whose language is pure and clean, uncon-
sciously she will mold her life like to those
portrayed in the books she reads; but if her
book friends are the giddy, impure, unchaste
kind, you may be certain that the girl will
become like them.

I have heard the assertion that to go to any
girl's bookcase and there study for a little
while the books she reads will give to one a
true estimate of that girl's character, and I
believe this is in the main true.

If a girl is interested in history she may
have at her command the works of educated
men who have made history a special study,
and there she may seek out just what they have
learned on the particular point that interests
her. If she is interested in science, medicine,
art, chemistry, music, or business in books she
can find the thoughts and conclusions of those
who have made these a life study.

Every girl likes in one way or another the
social side of life. By going to the proper kind
of authors she may get glimpses of and even
come into intimate acquaintance with the
lives of the purest and noblest of earth. She
can through her book friends converse with
people of the highest and noblest ideals. Or
she may seek out those whose lives are foul

and bitter and enter with them into their dark deeds, smudging her young heart with the worst sins of the world.

I believe every girl would be able to choose rightly if, when she begins a book, she would ask herself these questions: Would I like to read this book aloud to my mother? Would I feel honored in intimately knowing the people of this book in real life? Would pure society approve of the conduct of these story people? Can I profitably make my life pattern after the ideals I here find? Would the reading of this book help me to better serve my Lord? If these questions can be answered in the affirmative, then she may safely read the book; but if not, even though the book is very enticing, let her put it away, for it is poison.

The reading of love stories in which the lovers have secret meetings in dark and lonely places, freely embrace and caress each other, and whose acts and problems stir the fever of romance and imagination of the reader, is very detrimental to young girls, and is good for no one. Also detective stories that give real thrills, and stories of murder and crime, are poison to the morals of young people. It is almost as bad to read such books as to make personal friends with people who live such lives. In both you learn their intimate thoughts and motives and will condone their wrongs if their personality has appealed to you. More or less, my young reader, you will be like people whom you admire and like to read about.

Light, frivolous reading brings the brain into a condition where it is almost impossible for it to grasp and hold weighty matter. When the girl who habitually reads novels undertakes to read anything that requires thought, she seems to be only uttering words, and not comprehending a thing. She will throw the book down and say, "It is not interesting, and I see nothing in it." But let her keep at the heavier reading, going over and over the same paragraph or chapter till she does understand it—she will in time become able to grasp the thoughts as she reads. And if she keeps on at the deep reading, she will lose her appetite for the light stuff; it will seem chaffy and foolish to her.

It will not hurt any girl to read a few stories, and, in fact, if the right kind of stories are chosen she will learn much that is useful and good through story reading. But she who wishes to become educated and make her reading a means of culture must select the greater portion of her books from those authors who deal with facts in life. Works of history, biography, and other branches of learning are good for all. Books of travel are very good, for they make one acquainted with the people of other lands. In the great field of choice, pick out those book friends that will widen the outlook and lift up the standards of life.

Books can be the greatest of blessing in the life of a girl, or they can become her curse. Which will you have them to be in yours?

CHAPTER TWENTY-FIVE

WAKING OF THE LOVE-NATURE

Love is of God.

Every real woman loves. Her first love is that of the little child for its mother. Once, to lie in her mother's arms and to look up into the dear face filled all her little heart. After a while she was conscious of her father and her brother and sisters, and gradually they began to fill a large place in her affections. By and by her widening circle of love took in her little friends, and older people who were kind to her, until at last the schoolgirl of ten or twelve, if her childhood had been what it should have been, stood at the door of beautiful girlhood with a wealth of love in her own heart, and with just as bountiful a measure of love bestowed upon her by others.

It is at this time that another love-nature begins to waken, something the little girl has heard about, but never has felt before. The cause of this awakening lies in the changes that are taking place in her body. Organs that have been asleep all these years begin now to rouse from their stupor and to stir into growth and action, her whole body grows very rapidly and takes on a new form, and new feelings and emotions thrill her very soul.

This change in the body is so rapid, and it affects the disposition so greatly, that the girl gets all out of harmony with herself. It is as if she should come home some evening, to the very house where she had been living all the time, and, going in, should find the rugs and curtains all changed and considerable new furniture sitting about, but nobody present to tell her what it all meant.

How bewildered she would feel as she stood for a while trying to understand, and how awkward and confused she would feel. At such a time she would very likely call out for her mother, that she might understand the changes that had taken place in the home.

Just so it is with the girl of twelve or thirteen. It is her same body, she is herself, but for reasons that she cannot fathom everything seems different. New feelings and emotions have come into her heart like new furniture, while her love for her dolls and many childish games seem to have been set back out of the way. If the girl at this time will call out to her mother for explanation and guidance, she will get along all right, but some girls turn resolutely from their mother just now when they need her most and get themselves into tangles that almost spoil their young lives.

One of the strongest new emotions that come to furnish this house the girl is to live in is her new love-nature. By this nature I mean that affection which comes between boys and girls, and which is meant in time to prepare them to properly choose a companion for life. The effects of this awakening are peculiar. The boy becomes bashful and painfully self-conscious. He feels awkward and ill at ease and has a great dread of strangers, especially if they are women or girls, keeping himself out of sight at such times as much as possible. The girl, on the other hand, is liable to be more bold, and you will see her, if she is not properly guided by a wise mother, doing many things that are bold and daring. She dresses her hair in new and extravagant ways, is very particular about her dress, and studies her face to make it as beautiful as possible, all that she may be attractive and pleasing. Often she is unconscious that her attitude toward the boys has anything to do with her extreme care as to appearance, but it has a great deal to do with it. Her new nature is waking.

This new love-nature wants someone to love and is soon reaching out to find that one; but it is not wise to allow it to have its own way, or the purpose of God will be frustrated. This nature is intended to assist in the choice of a lifemate when the girl has grown older. Now it should be guarded carefully and allowed to grow and develop until the girl is capable of loving in a true, womanly manner. It is impossible to understandingly choose for life while yet in extreme youth, and those who are wise wait till they are older.

If girls allow themselves to fancy they are in love when they are yet very young, they will form extreme attachments, imagining they are desperately in love, only to have this passion pass away to give place to a new fancy. Thus in a few years the store of love that should have been saved till the good time when they should have a husband and home is frittered away on this one and that, and they are left almost without ability to love.

This new nature that is waking should be thought of as a beautiful plant given of God to be protected and cherished till it has become large and strong. If you had a delicate house-plant that was meant to be handled carefully and kept from the wind and heat, would you not be foolish to carry it out with you exhibiting it to everyone you met, letting it feel the hot sun, the sharp wind, and even the bitter cold? Your plant would either soon die entirely or be stunted and never become perfect in beauty. So it is with this new nature within you. If it is kept carefully as a sacred trust, it will grow into strong, warm affection that will be a rich store of joy and happiness for you by and by, but if brought out now and allowed to go to this one and that one it will wear itself away and lose its warmth and ardor.

Mary Wells often felt that her life was made hard because she was not allowed to go into young company as Bessie Wilson did. They were about the same age, neither of the girls being yet sixteen. Mary was treated as a little girl in that she seldom was allowed out at night, never "went with the boys," was kept regularly in school, and was referred to as Mr. Wells's little daughter. Bessie, on the other hand, dressed like a young woman, was often out to parties and theaters, had a sweetheart, and passed among the older girls as one of them. In school Mary was ahead of Bessie, who was just ready to quit because she was "tired of school" and had so little time for it.

"Papa," said Mary one day, "I am as old as Bessie Wilson, I am in a higher class in school, and I am as tall as she is, yet I may never do the things she does but have to look and act like a child. When are you going to let me grow up?"

"Mary, do you remember that lily that blossomed here in the window so early this spring?"

"Yes, but it is dead now. It seemed to give its whole strength to make that one blossom. It looked pretty then, but really those which blossomed at the right time were prettier," said Mary.

"That is just what I wanted you to remember. That lily was pretty, but it was forced along too fast, blossomed before its time, and died. That is the way with many girls. They blossom before their time. I want my daughter to come to her full, mature beauty."

"Do you mean that Bessie is blossoming too young?" asked Mary.

"When you come to the fullness of your

youth, when you are like a rose in full bloom, poor Bessie will already be fading."

Mary said no more, but she watched, and her father's prophecy was true. When Mary came to the full beauty of her young womanhood, Bessie was already a disappointed young wife, with her health gone.

Girls who are guided properly through the age of first love are more strictly guarded by their parents than in their childhood, and are reserved and careful. It is not always easy for a girl to submit to the advice of Mother and Father, to keep out of the social whirl, to remain a little girl, to dress modestly and act as quietly as she should, but every girl who will bring herself into obedience now will have much to be thankful for in coming years. At no time in a girl's life does she need her mother's oversight as in those years when the love-nature is waking.

During these years, at least up till she is past sixteen, a girl should not go out alone with boy company, nor should she be one of a crowd of boys and girls out at night or off on a long hike or hayride unless they are properly chaperoned. All these safeguards about a girl are like a wall of protection to her.

"You act as though you cannot trust me,"

said one girl because her mother insisted that during these years she should be carefully guarded.

"I do trust you, Daughter, but I would not have you placed in a position in which I could not personally vouch for your conduct if any question should come up. You are not yet old enough to be safe in relying wholly on your own judgment."

Generally when a girl has passed her six-teenth birthday she begins to see things more clearly, is not so broken up in her nature, and possibly begins to understand what a blessing her mother's care has been to her. If she is a girl of ordinarily good judgment, she will in another year or two begin to look at things from the standpoint of a young woman, not with the excited eyes of a child.

CHAPTER TWENTY-SIX

BOYFRIENDS

Discretion shall preserve thee,
understanding shall keep thee.

It is a strange experience in the life of any girl when she begins to realize that there is a difference in the way she feels toward boys and girls. While she enjoys being with her girl friends, yet there is a peculiar enjoyment and exhilaration in the company that includes a few boys. When she was but ten she could be her happiest with never a boy about, and if they did come and wished to join in her play with the girls, she felt angry about it. She said they were always teasing and tormenting, and the girls were better off with the boys away. Now, since she is in her teens, the addition of a boy or two makes the company much more lively.

All through her early teens the girl is better

off with many friends, both of boys and girls. Her friendship with the boys should be frank and open, with nothing in it lover-like. This age is the "gang" age, and boys and girls like to run together in "bunches." Parties and picnics are much enjoyed, and the girl's home seems often to fairly ring with the good times she and her mates have.

These "good times" are all right if they are always carried on with some older person present. The parties and picnics, the hikes and hayrides should all include one or more persons who are older, and under whose charge the younger ones are. And it is better if a girl's own mother is always along. "Good times" that are spoiled by proper chaperoning are to be condemned always. I know sometimes it seems as though parents think their children will never grow up and keep looking after them till they are entirely through their teens, but in every case it is all the better for the young people.

It is right that the girl should have opportunity for this pleasant social life, and parents will give them the opportunity as far as they are able.

In these friendships that thus spring up between boys and girls, there should be nothing personal, but they should be just common to all. When the boy and girl in their early and middle teens begin to speak of each other and to act toward each other as if they were sweethearts, then friendship has given place to something that is very foolish and very dangerous. At that age neither of them has been wakened in the affections long enough to understand what they are about. True love does not begin that way; the feelings they have for each other are immature. Fruit that is immature we call green, and the same expression can rightly be given to young people who give way to this early, immature love. It is never beautiful, but always offensive and silly. Do not be guilty.

But if a girl can have jolly, frank friendship with her boy acquaintances, such as is open to every girl in school, and yet keep herself from forming any silly attachments, then she will have a chance to know boys as they are. She can see their faults and virtues in their true light. She can notice the difference between the boys who smoke and those who do not, between those who are coarse and vulgar in their speech and manners and those who are pure and clean, between those who respect women and girls and always treat them with deference and those who do not, and seeing these differences she can form her ideals of manhood and nobility.

Girls have more influence with boys than often they realize. A boy who is rough and rowdy in the presence of one girl will be gentlemanly when with another girl, all because of the girl. If she is "loud" and boisterous, and will laugh at his silly and offensive remarks, he will act on that level; but when he is with a girl who never smiles at that which is rude and vulgar, who is always quiet and modest in her way, he will act as he knows pleases her. He may *seem* to have the better time with the first girl, but he respects the other girl more. No girl is doing herself justice if she allows the boys any familiarities with her. She can so conduct herself that they will not be taking liberties. Girls should not scuffle with the boys, nor allow them to put their arms about them, to kiss them, nor to hold hands in a silly, sentimental way. Kissing games are foolish and harmful. It is not the proper thing for girls to be seeking, nor to be ready to receive, compliments from the boys. Be reserved and careful, and though you do not *seem* to be so popular as the forward, giddy girl who is always "cutting up" with the boys, you will have the respect of the best boys and young men, and she will not.

If girls could always wait till they are eighteen or twenty before they have steady company, or allow themselves to have a real sweetheart, they could choose much better, and would often save themselves from doing foolish and silly things.

It is not best for a girl to seek to be what is sometimes called "a good pal" with the boys, being interested most in boys' games and doings. Men and boys expect women and girls to be different from themselves, and when they find one who is always aping their ways and manners and acting as if trying to be one of them, it cheapens that girl and her sex in the boys' eyes. We do not like the "sissy" boy nor the "womanish" man, nor do they want us to act "mannish." A girl can be a good friend and an interested comrade with her brother and his boyfriends without in the least making herself "common."

CHAPTER TWENTY-SEVEN

THE GIRL WHO CAN BE TRUSTED

I have chosen the way of truth.

A girl who can be trusted! What a treasure she is! What a strength of character she has for her young life's beginning if she has learned to keep her word exactly, to be trustworthy!

But not every girl is naturally trustworthy. Many have to learn through bitter experience that it is better to be true to one's word, to stand by a promise, to be obedient when out of sight and hearing of those over her, than to choose a different path and take it secretly.

It was a scene not to be forgotten by any of the three. The mother sat directly in front of the fire, its faint flickers showing the troubled lines on her face. The father sat at her left hand, his face set sternly, for he was a man to resent the actions of anyone who brought anxiety to that dear face beside him. At her right in a little huddled heap was the young daughter. She had just passed her fourteenth birthday, and she was as troubled and in as great a turmoil as many another girl of that age has found herself. She had been taking things into her own hands and having "good times" that had come about through deception, but the owl-like eyes of her mother, who, like many other mothers, seemed to see what was done entirely in the dark, had found out all the winding paths she had taken, and now the escapades were to be laid bare before her father. She dreaded the ordeal, and already was beginning to see that deception in all its results was a very unhappy road to follow. Mother began, while she glanced sadly at the girl beside her, for she pitied Laura very much.

"Laura, I have asked Papa to talk with us this evening, because I feel that we must have his advice and help in our present perplexities. I am going to tell him what our difficulties are, tell him exactly what has happened, beginning back a few weeks, so that he can understand what has led up to our present trouble. I will tell it just as I think it is, and I want you to listen closely, and if I am not telling it as you know it to be, speak up, for we want Papa to understand clearly, so that he can judge rightly. I want to be absolutely fair with you, Child. I would not lay one ounce of blame on you that does not belong there, so be free to speak if I make any mistake."

Laura sank her fair head a little lower on her breast as her mother was speaking, and both the parents felt deep pity for her. It was not going to be easy to lay everything bare before even as kind a judge as her father.

Slowly then the mother began telling the whole thing, Laura's willfulness, her small and greater deceptions, her sauciness and anger when faced with evidences of these deceptions, her promises to do better all broken, and at last the escapade that had brought about the present crisis. The girl had thus far interrupted but once or twice, and then only to clear up some minor point.

"I gave her permission to spend the afternoon away from home a couple of days ago, and she returned just when I expected her, and reported the good time she had had, even giving some of the details of their games. But to my surprise I have learned that she was not where I thought she was at all, but had spent the time with a crowd of young people like herself gadding about. I have investigated as far as I can, and I find no evidence that she has done anything disgraceful or unladylike during the afternoon; but the fact that she was not where I thought she was, that she tried to deceive me when she came home by false-hoods of what had happened during the after-noon, and that when I began to face her with evidences of her deception she actually told more untruths to cover her fault, proves that she has not been trustworthy. I feel that all my props are gone and that I must hold her in the right path by my own force of will. I do not feel that she is really trying to help me.

"Papa, this is the way it looks to me, and I want Laura to understand it: While a girl is young she is liable to do many things that are not wise, because of her lack of judgment. But if she will be obedient to her parents in a few points, that she will go exactly where they say she may, and not off somewhere else, and will tell the truth just as it is when asked about occurrences while she is out, then they can be a guard for her. They will know at all times just where she is and what she is doing or has done. Then if any question comes up as to her conduct, they can give an answer to all who would censure her. But if the girl will not go where she promises to go, and is away somewhere else, out of their knowledge, or if she will not tell the truth when asked about what has happened, then she places herself where her parents can be no protection to her. Now, while I can easily believe that Laura went nowhere and acted in no way that might be a reproach in the eyes of the world, the fact yet remains that if any evil tale should be started about her behavior, no matter how vile the tale might be, my testimony would add to her shame, for even in court I should have to say that I did not know where she was, that she deceived me and told me untruths. Can we afford, can she afford, to have things thus? I confess that this is the most serious matter that I have ever faced in Laura's training. I must have help in some way to get this to her."

"Laura, has Mama told this just as it is?" asked her father.

"Yes Sir, I think she has, so far as I could see," answered she.

Then followed question after question until the father was satisfied in his own heart that his wife had searched the thing to the bottom. "Have you asked God to help you, Laura, in doing right?" he asked.

"No, I have thought I could behave myself

if I tried hard enough," she said.

"You have not been trying very hard, I fear. Now, Laura, we will have no more of this sort of thing. If you can behave by yourself, very well. I think you ought to ask God's help. But be that as it may, I give you one more chance to prove yourself. If you cannot master yourself, I will take a greater hand in it, for we will have the victory over this deception way. You must be true, and you can be."

"I will, Papa. I promise you that nothing like this will ever happen again, and you may depend upon me." There was a note in Laura's voice, now so free from sauciness and anger, so full of humility and purpose, that gave her parents hope.

"Come here, Laura," said her father, tears in his eyes as he saw her meekness.

She rose and went to his side. He drew her into his arms, and sitting there on his knee with her head on his shoulder she listened while he told her of all that she meant to his life and to her mother's, of the hopes and prayers that were wrapped about her, and how grieved they were at her fault, but that now they believed she meant to do better, to be a girl who could be trusted.

"I will, Papa, I will, and I will prove to you

that I can be true," she sobbed earnestly, with her arms about his neck.

"Then let us pray, and ask our God to bless and help us all," the father said.

After prayer she kissed her parents and went to her room, with a purpose born of a new insight into trustworthiness. Her lesson was not forgotten, and she became what she purposed in her heart to be, a girl who could be trusted.

CHAPTER TWENTY-EIGHT

GETTING READY FOR THE GREAT RESPONSIBILITY

*Many daughters have done virtuously,
but thou excellest them all.*

Most good girls become wives and mothers. There are some truehearted women who do not, but they will very nearly all tell you, as old age creeps on them, that they feel certain they have missed the best that life could have given them. One woman who had given her life in noble and uplifting work, whose name is familiar in every home for her influence in the lives of other women, said when questioned on this very point (for she never married), "I would give it all for the touch of little hands." There is a heart-cry in every woman that cannot be satisfied except in motherhood.

If a girl knew that she was to be a teacher, an artist, or a musician, she would not put off all thought and preparation for her lifework till she was ready to begin it, but instead would fit herself for it by study and practice. There would be years of hard work between her and success in her chosen calling.

There is no calling higher than that of motherhood, and the place of wife is nearly as high. The wife, if she is what God means for her to be, is a helpmeet, a strength and constant blessing to her husband. He is a better man with a fuller and more useful life because of her influence. Without her, his life could not be perfect. To be this to one person all through a lifetime may mean much to any woman. And by making his life fuller, her own life is enlarged, and others are blessed by them. It is a wonderful and a noble thing to be a good wife, and the mistress of a real home.

But the calling of a mother is yet higher. Then the woman brings into the world other beings and is responsible to God and to the world for their care and training. It is a life-long job, and one that will tell for good or bad to the end of the world. Not one woman who has been a mother has failed to leave her imprint on the world. There are now on record the names of women whose wicked lives and ungodly children and children's children down to the present generation have cost their states and cities thousands of dollars; and there are other women whose names are on record in life's history, whose godly and upright lives have so influenced their children, that they down to the present generation are a blessing and benediction in the world. Motherhood is a far-reaching destiny indeed. It is the highest calling, the noblest work, the greatest honor that can come to any woman. This is also what will, if used rightly, bring her the most happiness and genuine satisfaction of anything in life. For this God made her, and fitted her by nature.

Nature begins, when the girl is just entering her teens, to rapidly fit the girl's body for motherhood. Those organs that are especially given for that work begin to grow and develop, and the nature of the girl begins to change, as we have shown, to make her ready to desire and appreciate her calling when the right time comes. This bodily change is not completed so that the girl is ready for her wonderful work till she has finished her teens. There are a few girls who develop into full womanhood before they are twenty, but they are not many among us, and some are not mature until several years above twenty. There are six to ten years of life given by nature to this special work in the body, and if she is not hindered she will give her child a beautiful "temple of health" in which to live and fulfil her lifework. But many girls strive against the design of wise Mother Nature, to their own sorrow.

The wise girl will dress in proper clothing, so that her body will not be bound and choked in its efforts to develop; her clothing will also be sufficient to protect her from cold and dampness, so that no shock shall hinder nature in her work; the girl will take proper exercise in the open air so that her muscles will develop and her lungs can be filled with the life-giving oxygen, for nature never meant that her children should be hothouse plants; she will eat properly and regularly, not making her stomach a dumping-ground for all the foolish likes and fancies of the palate; she will take a sufficient amount of sleep in a properly ventilated room, not keeping late hours either in retiring or rising; she will seek in all she does to live a quiet, simple, natural life, giving nature a chance to do her best. The keeping of these simple rules of health will be of untold benefit, and their breaking may lead to lifelong regret.

The body is not the only part of a girl that should be fitted for the duties of womanhood. The girl needs knowledge of many things. The responsibilities that will be hers as wife and mother go out in every direction, and she needs to learn to be an all-round woman.

First in importance in this consideration is the cultivation of her own nature so that she can be true in affection, steady in purpose, and reliable in responsibility. She needs to be able to control herself so that she can give up her way for the peace of her little realm, and be able to hold all the members of her kingdom through the bonds of love. The selfish and self-willed, the tempestuous and stormy, the indolent and sluggish, the careless and indifferent—all are out of the race. They can never make the best mothers. It takes real women to make good mothers, and real women can govern and direct their own actions aright.

The girl needs to have a working knowledge of the responsibilities that will be hers. She should know how to cook and bake, to wash and iron, to scrub and clean, to sew and mend—in fact, how to do everything that a housewife needs to have done. If her circumstances are such that she does not actually have this work to do, she can direct the efforts of others the better for knowing how the work is done.

The girl should know how to buy economically, both for the kitchen and household, and for the wardrobe. Without this knowledge she will waste her husband's means and make his path hard in the beginning of their lives together. This knowledge should be gained at home, where she can have practical experience. She should be able to keep within a set margin of expenses, not buying recklessly.

Last of all—but far from least—the girl should learn to love little children and to make them her friends. She ought to learn how to care for infants, and how to build up in her heart a desire for motherhood. No, my girls, it is not a thing to be ashamed of, that desire in you for little children. God put it there, and if you really feel, as some girls will lightly say of themselves, that you never want to be bothered with babies, then you are an unnatural girl. Somewhere poison has been put into your mind and heart, which should be purged out, and right principles of life implanted instead.

Getting ready for womanhood is serious business, and not to be taken lightly. Every girl should have a thorough knowledge of herself and of the proper care of her body. There are books that treat on this very subject, and from them every girl can learn what she needs and really desires to know about herself.

The real woman's life is so filled with love and gladness that all the suffering and pain that must come as a portion of motherhood is forgotten in the joy it brings. May God bless the dear mothers to be, and help them to get ready for the work that will be theirs.

CHAPTER TWENTY-NINE

CHOOSING A LIFEWORK

She layeth her hands to the spindle,
and her hands hold the distaff.

Every girl should be able to make her own living if it becomes necessary. It is not wise for every girl to go out into the working world and there contend for her own livelihood, for many homes need the services of a loving daughter more than she needs the extra spending money that her work will bring. More unwise yet is it for women who should be housekeepers and homemakers to give their homes over to the hands of servants or close their doors altogether, to go forth to earn money for the money's sake. But there are many women and girls whose circumstance compel them to be breadwinners, and not one girl knows that such will not sometime be her lot.

The field from which a girl may choose

her lifework is much wider than once it was. In the days of our grandmothers' youth the girl who was forced to earn her livelihood had only two or three vocations to choose from beyond that of a house servant; but the girl of today has almost as wide a choice as her brother, for nearly every vocation that is open to him is also open to her. The act of choice therefore becomes harder, and more depends upon the girl herself.

If circumstances are such that the girl should stay in her own home and not become one of the breadwinners of the day, she should if possible prepare herself in some particular way so that in case of future need she could use her knowledge for gain.

There are many things to be taken into consideration by the girl who is making choice of her lifework. She wants to make a success, not only in her work, but in her life, so that as much good as possible will be the result of her having lived.

The first consideration with any girl is no doubt her own desires and tastes. What would be pleasure to one would be irksomeness to another, and no one can do her best at what is always unpleasant. Her next consideration will be her ability to do what she wants to do. Has she talent for that particular work? Are her health and physical strength sufficient to warrant her undertaking it? It would be foolish to give time and means in preparing for that for which one is naturally unfitted.

Another point to consider seriously is the associations into which her choice would lead her. She must remember that to fill her place in life she must be first of all a woman, with all that that can mean, and to undertake any work that would make her less womanly, less able to fill the ideals of real womanhood, would be both unwise and sinful. There are many things that a woman *could* do, but which in doing she would be thrown into company with all kinds of men in a way so intimate that she could keep neither their respect nor her own. Such a choice would be madness, for she would be destroying what in woman is the most beautiful—modesty and purity.

A work, to be worthy of a choice, should be needful, uplifting, and noble. No other choice is worthy the consideration of any girl. She should ask herself seriously: *Will this work I intend to do make the world better, or help in any of its necessary toil? Shall I, in doing it, be doing my part in lifting the burdens of life? Will it make me a better woman for the doing, or at least leave me as good a woman as I am?*

Life is not all made up of pleasure and frolic, and our work should be something that is of real service.

There is no work that is worthwhile and yet learned and performed without effort. Sluggards never make successes anywhere. The girl who would win for herself a place in the earning world must be ready to work long and hard.

There is no nobler profession for any girl to chose than that of a teacher. Her years of preparation will be filled with hard work and persistent efforts, and the performing of that work is both wearing and vexing, but the results can be great. Not only should the teacher guide her pupils in paths of knowledge, but also into ways of truth and uprightness. Her moral and spiritual influence can be great for good in the schoolroom, if she properly prepares herself for it, and performs her work with the highest aims in view.

The artist and musician can bring much pleasure and happiness into the world through their gifts, happiness that need stir only the best that is in men and women. But this work is perfect only after long effort and persistent application.

The writer of books and short stories has a field before her which, followed in the right direction, can do much good in the world—but which, followed in another direction, will add only to the curse that is already in the world. The wrong kinds of stories are better never written. The writer also meets much difficulty in getting started in life. Many who try never succeed. It is at best a long, hard way, but one that is pleasant indeed to follow by those who love to do that kind of work.

There are many openings for a girl in the business world that she can fill without detracting from her womanliness, if she will. Though it takes less preparation for business in the beginning, the work itself is one long school of hard work.

There is another class into which many young girls are forced by circumstances, work that makes them a living, and is honest enough, but which will not show the personality of the girl herself as do the professions I have been mentioning, and that work is such as is found in the factory, shop, or store. The girl who must do this kind of work can do well what she does, can fill a worthy place. But in the majority of cases the girls found here are doing only such work till the time when they shall go to life's greatest responsibility, the making of a home.

There is a strong prejudice against the doing of the housework for a living. This arises no doubt from the idea of servitude, but all work is service of one kind or another. There is no work that is more necessary or capable of bringing more real pleasure than housework. Any girl who can do this work well need not be ashamed of her calling. If she uses the spare moments she can find for study and reading, she need not let her mind starve, and become but a drudge, because this is her calling. All needful work is honorable if it is done well and for a good purpose.

A mistake that many girls make who must go out to work is that of neglect of home duties. They allow themselves to go on from year to year with no knowledge of household work. They cannot cook a good meal, nor make a garment; it would be impossible for them to do a washing and ironing properly, both for lack of skill and because of fatigue. Such girls, many of whom can hope to marry only poor men who are able to give them but a small allowance for household purposes, come to marriage without any knowledge of housework, or of the buying value of money.

Here is the cause of many home wrecks. Every girl should remember that first of all she is a woman, and the woman in her will desire and claim a home for her own some day, and if she is to be a success there she must make some preparation for that calling.

CHAPTER THIRTY

A CONSECRATED LIFE

I have chosen you, and ordained you,
that ye should go and bring forth fruit.

There is no life so unhappy and discontented as one that is aimless. For any life to be satisfying it must have a goal that leads the path upward. Some people indeed succeed in what they undertake, but their goal is so low that when they accomplish their aim it is as bad as a failure could have been. To one who aims low, or not at all, *success* can never come, for it is only when we approach near to what God intended we should be, the very best that is in us, that *real success* can be attained. Success can mean nothing less than the accomplishment of good.

Though one might hitch her "wagon to a star," so high and noble are her aspirations, yet if after all that star is an earthly one—

knowledge, personal influence, ability, riches, honor—and her aspirations be realized and she arise high in the world, she will not find the satisfaction in her attainments that she hoped for. We, in our natures, are not altogether earthy; there is in us a nature that craves to be in tune with heaven. A life that gives exercise to this part of our being and provides a way for the satisfying of the heart's craving for God is the only one that brings what every person desires—soul rest. That is why I wish to talk to you about the consecrated life, the life all given in humble, willing service to God.

Under the old Mosaic law, one tribe of the children of Israel was chosen for the service of God in a peculiar sense, and they were set apart from the rest for that purpose. Out of that tribe the priestly family was chosen, and they were to serve at the altar and in the tabernacle. The vessels that were used about the altar and everything consecrated to the temple service were to be used for that purpose only, and if in any way they became unfit for that service they were destroyed; never were they used part of the time for common purpose.

Our service now is not according to that old, formal worship, for now hearts and affections are asked in consecration, not pots and pans. Then the service of God consisted to a great extent in the proper keeping of certain forms and ceremonies; now the service of God is counted only that devotion which comes from a sincere and consecrated heart. The consecration of earthly vessels then is a picture of the complete consecration of heart now, for we are to be fully the Lord's for all time, not giving a portion of our time and affection to the world and sin, and to the following of selfish purposes. Every act of life, every thought of the heart, every affection of the soul, all for God and done in the glory of God.

This consecrated life is expected of every Christian. In fact, no person can live a conscientious, Christian life long without finding such a consecration necessary. Either he must give himself fully to God, or drop back into the cold, formal life that many live, but none enjoy. Do not let anyone think that such a devoted life is irksome, for it is not. We are so created that the heart naturally craves God, and when the powers of sin that bind have been broken and the soul has been set free to follow its right course, the highest pleasure is found in sincere service to God.

Out of the ranks of those who fully follow Him, God chooses some whom He sees in His wisdom could particularly glorify Him in special service, and these He calls to the work He would have them to do. To such there comes a conviction of heart, an inward knowledge, that makes them know they are set apart for special service.

There are many kinds of work that are in a peculiar sense the Lord's. Work among the poor and needy, visiting them, and ministering to their wants, especially to the sick and helpless among them, is to be found almost everywhere, and for those who will do this work humbly and gladly there is a rich reward in heaven. One of the tests put to true religion is, Has he who professes to possess it visited the fatherless and widow in their affliction? To think that we can be Christians and shut our hearts against those who are in need shows that the first principles of true Christianity have not been learned by us.

Again, there is the ministry of song, when the voice which God has given is used to win souls to God and to encourage those who are cast down. This is a wonderful and noble work.

Some are called to preach the gospel. Once it was thought that this was not a proper calling for women, but God uses those whom He finds suited to the work and willing to do His bidding. There is great responsibility in this calling, and much fortitude and earnestness are needed to make this calling successful in the fullest sense.

Most noble and wonderful of all is the calling or work of a missionary. There are many departments of this work for which women are especially fitted, and there is ever room for more persons willing to literally leave all to follow Jesus. In no other calling can one so fully give all for Jesus. To be successful in this field years of hard work are necessary, and some must lay down their lives on the battlefield. The call is for consecrated workers. Whether home missionaries, gospel workers, or missionaries to foreign lands, from all God wants consecrated and willing service.

The one who is thus called, and accepts the call, must expect a long, and in some respects a difficult, preparation. Those vessels that are the most precious are often the longest in the hands of the potter, and the processes through which they must pass the most severe. The one who is to stand before the people as an example of the grace of God, a pattern for others to follow, must expect to be made like the great pattern.

Preparation for God's work is, on our part, of two kinds—that which is acquired through study and application, and that which is learned in the school of experience.

My dear girl, if deep in your heart of hearts you feel that God is calling you, that you should dedicate your life to the work of God, then turn your face resolutely to the things of God. Study the Word of God, and all other books that will give you the knowledge you will need for your work. If possible, go to some school where you can yet better prepare yourself, all the while keeping ready to do the little things for God that you find need doing by the way.

Besides this, live close to God in prayer, fighting your life battles through, seeking in everything to follow the guiding of the Lord. To you will come many experiences that will test your grace and fortitude, many temptations to try you, that you may prove your strength and courage, and that you may know the battles that others have to fight.

If God has called you to His work, look not upon it as a hardship, but go forth gladly, willing and ready to go and to suffer and die for the cause you love. From your ranks, you are girls now, God will call many for service.

Let Him find willing servants, who will fully yield their whole lives to Him.

But I would not forget the rank and file, those who are not specially called, but whose lives are set in the ordinary channels, who are to make the home women of our land. Let not one think that only in special service is consecration needed. Every act of our lives can be service to God. She who makes a good home, where others are encouraged and strengthened, she who is ready to speak a kind and encouraging word to those in need, she who keeps up a humble and quiet everyday service to God—she is glorifying Him just as much as are they who go on special missions.

CHAPTER THIRTY-ONE

A PURE HEART

Blessed are the pure in heart:
for they shall see God.

What a pleasure to look forth upon the bosom of the earth on a clear morning after a snowstorm, when over all is spread the covering of pure whiteness, hiding every defect and blemish, surmounting all that is unclean and ugly, transforming every stick and clod into things of beauty, leaving only blue sky above and pure whiteness below! Or what a pleasure to stand at the brink of a clear, calm pool, looking into its depths without observing one thing unclean, and then to put to your lips a cup of the crystal liquid fresh from the spring that feeds the pool, and drink to your fill!

What a sense of the infinite one feels standing on the top of the mountain height far above the dust and smoke of the lower regions, and there drinking in the pure air, and gazing as far as the eye can carry in every direction, the sight unobstructed by the thickness and gloom of lower levels! Or, again, what a sense of the infinite one feels out under the clear sky, there beholding the stars shining forth with all their beauty and brightness, pure revelations of the mighty power of God!

To look into the depths of a child's innocent eyes and see there but the innocence and guiltlessness of one who has never sinned will soften the hard heart. To look into the clear, fearless eye of the man or woman whose heart is free from condemnation of sin, or to see the quietness and confidence of old age that has come to its own with cleanness of hands and purity of heart, gives strength to those who falter. The look of innocent pleasure in the eyes of a modest maiden gladdens all who behold it.

Everywhere purity and cleanness are admired and appreciated. Pure air, pure water, pure food, pure associations, pure ideals, pure aspirations—all are needed for perfect living.

The purity that counts for most in your life and mine is purity of heart. It is possible for us to live with the very seat of our affections cleansed from that which is sinful, and our hearts made pure. The heart can be made a fit temple into which to ask the Lord to come and be the inhabitant.

One of the things every young Christian girl soon becomes aware of is the natural sinfulness of her own heart. When she is trying to do that which is right, evil thoughts and feelings will arise. She is tempted to be proud and selfish, and under certain provocation she feels the workings of anger in her heart, though by looking to God for help she keeps her lips from speaking out her feelings. Sometimes she is startled by feelings of jealousy and envy, two things that must not be allowed in the life of a Christian. She will find it hard at times to follow the Lord fully, to entirely do His will. If she will seek out the real desire of her heart, she will find that she wants a closer walk with God, yet when she tries to walk closer she is all the more conscious of these sinful impulses. If she understood herself she would know she needed a pure heart.

If a girl will come to God with her perplexities and tell Him the struggle she is having with "foes within," and fully consecrate her life to Him, saying from the depth of her heart, "Lord, I give my life to Thee. Thou mayest have every part of it. Cleanse my heart and make it a fit place for Thee to dwell," and trusting God to do what she has asked Him to do, she may have a pure heart.

God will cleanse out those sinful principles from her nature and make her a conqueror. Not that she will no more be tempted, but instead of those inward struggles that are so hard to master, she will find inward grace and strength to overcome.

There is a heavenly visitor who will come in and fill the heart that is fully given to God, so that instead of sinful impulses ruling there, this sweet Spirit of God will reign.

The experience of heart-purity is not for anyone who *cherishes* any thought or feeling that is impure. If envy, or jealousy, or pride, or arrogance, or any kindred evil is allowed a place, the Spirit of God will not come to cleanse and fill His temple.

It seems to me a most wonderful thing, this deliberate giving over of oneself and life for God alone. We think of the young nun who leaves all the world and takes the veil for life, and wonder at her fortitude, and bewail her needless sacrifice, but on the other hand we too often fail to see that there is consecration and sacrifice in genuine Christian service. Not that sacrifice which in a sense buries one alive, but the consecration of service that will allow no desire or thought or aspiration to linger that is known to be contrary to the will of God.

There is a rest of spirit, and a quiet confidence, a joyfulness, and a perfection of love and peace in the heart of the one thus given over to God that cannot be described in words. Nor is this experience for only a favored few. Everyone who will seek God with all his heart, who will draw close, may have this experience of a pure heart.

CHAPTER THIRTY-TWO

A FEW FAULTS DISCUSSED

*To him that overcometh will I give
to eat of the hidden manna.*

There are none among us who can truthfully boast of faultlessness. I wish to speak particularly now to those who are earnestly endeavoring to live a Christian life. Such girls will have seasons of inward searchings and examinations that will bring them face-to-face with their own shortcomings and weaknesses. What shall they do with them?

There is the fault of irresolution. A person, to be of strong character, must be able to make up his mind, to make decisions, and to stand by those decisions in the face of hindrances and opposition. He who is irresolute is not sure of himself. He is ever going back to see whether or not he made a mistake in his decision. We have read of the character in

Pilgrim's Progress who saw lions in the way and was not strong enough to march up to them. They who did face their lions found them bound so that they could not reach the path. But he who is irresolute never gets that far.

The girl who has acquired this habit of halting between opinions, of never making up her mind on anything, needs to take herself in hand sternly, look problems in the face, march right out to meet them, and fight her own battles through. To the one who is determined to win, victory will come.

Self-consciousness is a sister of irresolution. She causes her victim to keep his eyes on only himself, to study his own thoughts and feelings and acts, and to look to condemn. When he goes into the company of others, he feels that all eyes are upon him; when he undertakes to do anything, he is conscious of his every word and act, and, blushing, stammering, apologizing, he succeeds in doing just the thing he hates—getting eyes upon himself.

The girl who is self-conscious needs to begin doing something for others. If you go into company, seek out someone who needs encouragement, a helping hand, and give it. Possibly you will see another more miserably embarrassed than you are; if so, help that one.

There is no other cure for self-consciousness like keeping busy and interested in others. Those terrible feelings come only to those who have time to entertain them.

Here is a girl whose besetting fault is sharpness of speech. It may come from nervousness of temperament, from environment, or from some other cause, but no matter what the cause, the result is always the same, hurting and wounding those who hear. Such a girl needs first of all to guard her thoughts. "Out of the abundance of the heart the mouth speaketh." If sharp, critical thoughts are allowed, then sharp, critical words will be the result. If we will form the habit of watching for good things in others and of speaking about them, kindness will become a habit.

Another fault is an inordinate love for pretty things. I say "inordinate," for there is a proper appreciation for those things that are beautiful that is allowable in everyone. But she who has too great a love for these things sets great value upon their possession. Pride and vanity follow close in the wake of a love for personal adornment. Money that should go for more necessary things is given for things beautiful. The girl becomes dissatisfied with the home and surroundings as she finds them, developing a deep dislike for what should be dear to her, all because they do not meet her ideal of beauty.

Such a girl needs to learn to look well to the good that is about her. Where love is, real beauty can be found. There is nothing more beautiful than a happy, satisfied heart. If your love for pretty things so fills your heart that you cannot see the good that loving hands and hearts would bring to you, then you need to give serious attention to that which is obstructing your vision.

There is a spirit of discontent that makes the girl restless and uneasy. Now, I would not have you fully satisfied with things just as they are, so that you will not strive to improve, but that dissatisfaction that keeps a girl fretting about her fate spoils her happiness now and unfits her to appreciate what may be in the future.

Selfishness is another fault that spoils the beauty of many lives. He who is selfish looks always to his own pleasure first. If others are displeased and inconvenienced, it matters little to him, if his own desires are met. This form of selfishness can creep into the lives of those who desire to serve God. I have seen girls who, though they were Christians, were so insistent about little things, so determined to have their own way, that they spoiled the beauty that Christ would have put into their lives.

This kind of selfishness will show out again in the way that a girl will enter into her church work. She can become so engrossed with her Sunday school, or league, or her attendance at the general services, that her presence there or her time given to work for her beloved church may mean the robbing of her mother of opportunity to get out at all. It is pitiful to see a girl engaged in even a good cause if such continually keeps her mother or sister at home with the cares found there. A fair division is the right thing under such circumstances.

Again, selfishness will show out in the fact that the girl's clothes are so much nicer and more up-to-date than what her mother wears. It may be that Mother is willing for her daughter to have the best, but that does not change the fact that the daughter is selfish if she takes the best always.

Sensitiveness is another great fault. Dema, a young woman of beautiful character, had sensitiveness as a besetting fault. At the least rebuke or criticism she would become so hurt and mortified that she would weep for hours, and many times when the speaker had not thought of bruising her at all, she would suffer greatly with wounded feelings. She was visiting for some time in the home of a gentleman who was able to see the beauty of her character in spite of this outstanding fault. One day she had wept till her eyes were red over something that had not been intended as a thrust at her at all. When she reappeared in the family circle, he watched her closely, and finding her alone, he called her attention to a sensitive plant growing outside the window.

"If I should touch that plant ever so lightly, Dema, what would be the result?" he asked.

"I have often watched it," she replied, "and touched it just to see its behavior. It will close up every leaf upon the whole plant and remain just so till it has recovered from the shock of my gentlest touch. It is called rightly a sensitive plant."

"Dema, you are our sensitive plant. We have to be as careful in handling you as if you were indeed just such a plant. We should enjoy you much more if you were not so sensitive."

The fountain of tears again burst forth as poor Dema saw herself pictured by the little plant, but going to her room she asked God to help her to overcome. Such earnest prayers do not go unanswered, especially when the supplicant is willing, as was Dema, to fight against the weakness.

There are many faults, but every one of them can be overcome if the girl sets her heart to be victorious.

CHAPTER THIRTY-THREE

THE FULL-BLOWN ROSE

Strength and honour are her clothing.

A thing of beauty is a rose in full bloom. What a pleasure to hold in the hand a perfect rose and admire its soft, velvety petals, to smell of its rich fragrance, and to feast upon its beauty of coloring! One would be tempted to say, "In this nature had done her best." But nature, and the God of nature, gives us many beautiful and glorious things.

After the uncertainties of girlhood, when the crudeness and lack of symmetry in body and mind have been put away and the woman of promise is before us in all her beauty and grace, we are privileged to see in her who was once the girl one of the most blessed of God's creation, a good, true woman. Just such a fulfillment of hope and expectancy every true mother wants in her daughter.

The grown woman who stands just at the door of life's responsibilities ready to enter in upon her lifework represents powers and possibilities unbounded. Her influence in the world is sure to go on down to the end of time. It is impossible that she should live entirely for and to herself.

First is her influence upon womankind. There are none of us so weak and insignificant but what someone will pattern after us or draw courage from us. By our trueness to principle, our loyalty to right and truth, we can each be a stay and fortress to the weaker sisters about us. In the home, in the neighborhood, in the congregation, everywhere, a good woman is a mighty force among women. And just as powerful is the influence of a woman who is not good. It lies in the power of woman to lift up, and terribly in her power to pull down and destroy.

The woman has influence unbounded with mankind. A good woman can be like a star of hope, a beacon light, a safe retreat, to the man who is struggling against the obstacles of the world. In her he can see the ideal of purity and truth, and the manhood in him will strive to be worthy of her. But if she steps down from the path of true, virtuous womanhood and becomes petty or sinful, she will be his downfall. There is no true woman who does not know that in a great measure she is her brother's keeper.

Then comes the influence of a true woman upon the youth of her acquaintance. It may be that the boys and girls about her seem to be full of nonsense and foolishness, that they do not see her example of earnest, lovely nobility, but in a few years more she will see that her life does bear fruit among those with whom she associates. Every girl has her ideal woman, and that woman is picked from among her acquaintances. No woman can live to herself.

If the influence of a bad woman is great among her sisters and yet more so among her brothers, it is far worse among the young. A woman with a sweet, smiling face and a heart that is unclean is as great a curse as can come into the life of either a boy or girl.

Oh, girls! girls! life is so great, so wonderful, so full of possibilities, that none of us can afford to be anything but what is good and pure and true! Let us make the perfect rose an emblem of our womanhood and strive that its fragrance shall bless all who come in contact with it.

Inspirational Library

Beautiful purse/pocket-size editions of Christian classics bou
in flexible leatherette. These books make thoughtful gifts f
everyone on your list, including yourself!

When I'm on My Knees The highly popular collection of devotional thoughts on prayer, especially for women.
Flexible Leatherette. $4.97

The Bible Promise Book Over 1,000 promises from God's Word arranged by topic. What does God promise about matters like: Anger, Illness, Jealousy, Love, Money, Old Age, and Mercy? Find out in this book!
Flexible Leatherette. $3.97

Daily Wisdom for Women A daily devotional for women seeking biblical wisdom to apply to their lives. Scripture taken from the New American Standard Version of the Bible.
Flexible Leatherette. $4.97

My Daily Prayer Journal Each page is dated and features a Scripture verse and ample room for you to record your thoughts, prayers, and praises. One page for each day of the year.
Flexible Leatherette. $4.97

Available wherever books are sold.
Or order from:

Barbour Publishing, Inc.
P.O. Box 719
Uhrichsville, OH 44683
http://www.barbourbooks.com

If you order by mail, add $2.00 to your order for shipping.
Prices are subject to change without notice.